DRINKING, DRUG USE, AND ADDICTION IN THE AUTISM COMMUNITY

of related interest

Asperger Syndrome and Alcohol
Drinking to Cope?
Matthew Tinsley and Sarah Hendrickx
ISBN 978 1 84310 609 8
eISBN 978 1 84642 814 2

Realizing the College Dream with Autism or Asperger Syndrome
A Parent's Guide to Student Success
Ann Palmer
ISBN 978 1 84310 801 6
eISBN 978 1 84642 250 8

A Friend's and Relative's Guide to Supporting the Family with Autism
How Can I Help?
Ann Palmer
ISBN 978 1 84905 877 3
eISBN 978 0 85700 567 0

Parenting Across the Autism Spectrum
Unexpected Lessons We Have Learned
Maureen F. Morrell and Ann Palmer
ISBN 978 1 84310 807 8
eISBN 978 1 84642 506 6

DRINKING, DRUG USE, AND *ADDICTION* IN THE AUTISM COMMUNITY

Elizabeth Kunreuther and Ann Palmer

Foreword by Tony Attwood

Jessica Kingsley *Publishers*
London and Philadelphia

First published in 2018
by Jessica Kingsley Publishers
73 Collier Street
London N1 9BE, UK
and
400 Market Street, Suite 400
Philadelphia, PA 19106, USA

www.jkp.com

Library of Congress Cataloging in Publication Data
A CIP catalog record for this book is available from the Library of Congress

British Library Cataloguing in Publication Data
A CIP catalogue record for this book is available from the British Library

ISBN 978 1 78592 749 2
eISBN 978 1 78450 539 4

Printed and bound in Great Britain

CONTENTS

FOREWORD

Tony Atwood

I was delighted to be invited to write a foreword to this book, as I have long recognised the high level of addiction in those who have an ASD, from both my professional and personal experience, having members of my own family who have an ASD and addiction.

It used to be assumed that those who have an Autism Spectrum Disorder are not at greater risk of developing an addiction than those with any other developmental disorder. However, in my own clinical practice. I have seen an increasing number of adolescents and adults with ASD who have signs of addiction, primarily alcohol and drug dependency, and excessive time engaged in computer games. The question has then arisen as to why someone with an ASD is predisposed to develop such an addiction. The simple explanation is either to engage reality or to escape reality. To explain this seemingly contradictory statement, the specific characteristics of ASD need to be considered.

One fundamental characteristic of ASD is a difficulty socializing with, and being accepted by, peers. The machinery of social engagement creaks and squeaks, and alcohol and marijuana can act as social lubrication. The person with ASD may find socializing easier when mildly intoxicated; substances such as alcohol, marijuana and other drugs reduce social anxiety, and create a sense of relaxation and competence. Unfortunately, the person may then become dependent on these to facilitate any social engagement.

Another characteristic of ASD in adolescence is the tendency to be rejected by peers, engendering feelings of not belonging to any specific group or culture. The acquisition and consumption of alcohol and drugs—easily available and the "currency" of popularity and status—can provide membership of a sub-culture composed of others who also do not fit into conventional society. However, they do accept those who are different and marginalized. This sub-culture has clear rules and expectations in how to dress, talk and behave, and has its own language and rituals, "friendships" are formed, and the person is warmly welcomed, especially if he or she becomes a drug courier or supplier. Thus, for the wrong reasons, the person with an ASD belongs to a group and is accepted and valued by peers.

In the case of gaming, there can be an intense engagement, which provides a sense of achievement and identity, often through natural talent and considerable practice. The achievements in group player games on the Internet can lead to the person being popular with fellow gamers, who seek and admire his or her abilities, knowledge and guidance. When playing the game there is little, if any, social chit chat, and no requirement to process non-verbal communication or follow social conventions. The game provides excitement, respect and popularity, and becoming an avatar creates an enjoyable alternative reality.

Many of my clients describe trying to cope with racing thoughts, which are difficult to slow down, and ruminations that are extremely difficult to block. Alcohol and drugs can induce a deceleration of thoughts that are speeding out of control, and can stop ruminations. Computer games can also be a very effective thought blocker to both ruminations over past events, and persistent negative thoughts that lead to low self-esteem and depression. These games can also act as an energizer when the person is socially and emotionally exhausted.

We recognize that around 85 percent of those who have ASD also experience high levels of anxiety. Alcohol and drugs, both legal and illicit, can provide relief from constant feelings of anxiety. Some medications prescribed to reduce anxiety, such as the benzodiazepines, can themselves become addictive, with the person developing increased tolerance. There can also be a dangerous misuse of other prescription medications as the person self-medicates for anxiety, with the potential for a hazardous interaction of substances, and the very real risk of accidental overdose.

There are high levels of unemployment associated with ASD, leading to boredom, frustration and a sense of uselessness and under-achievement. Being part of the drug or gaming culture can provide purpose and structure for the day. There is a sense of achievement in seeking and finding drugs, and an opportunity to leave one's accommodation and to meet people. Completing the various levels of the computer game can also provide structure and achievement, and the development of expertise that is recognized and valued by fellow gamers.

The use of substances or engagement in computer games can provide a sense of protection, "anaesthetizing" the person from the effects of past trauma, such as being bullied, or being the victim of emotional, physical, financial or sexual abuse. The addiction may alleviate any feelings of depression about the past, the current situation and future prospects.

Thus, there are many reasons why someone who has an ASD is vulnerable to developing an addiction. The next question is what to do when there are signs of addiction.

The first stage is to recognize the addiction, which may be affecting mental and physical health, and sometimes, as in the case of substance abuse, leading to criminal activities to pay for the substances. The person who has the addiction may lack insight into the depth of the addiction, failing to recognize their inability to cope without mind-altering substances or access to gaming. If there is recognition of the addiction, there nevertheless may be resistance to reducing the level of substances or engagement, as the person may not be able to conceptualize life without their "prop".

The second stage is to address the dysfunctional use of substances and games. In the case of drugs, this may mean providing prescribed and carefully administered and supervised alternative medication. In the case of computer games, the amount of time gaming can be gradually reduced, and a wider range of activities encouraged, providing a sense of achievement and social engagement. Throughout this process, access to a clinical psychologist is beneficial, to provide advice, treatment and support for anxiety management, and to encourage the development of social skills and new social networks.

While the diagnosis of ASD may provide a rationalization for the addiction, it must also be considered when accessing support and therapy services. There will be those who enter the treatment services for addiction who have undiagnosed ASD; it is important that there is routine screening for ASD of all new participants in rehabilitation therapy and services for addiction, not only to determine the possible reasons for the addiction, but also, importantly, to modify the therapy according to the characteristics of ASD.

Rehabilitation services often rely on social living and group therapy and activities, and provide limited opportunities for personal space and solitude. The person with an ASD will benefit from a single room wherever possible. They will also need guidance and support in the social and disclosure requirements in group therapy. For example, there can be difficulties recognizing social and personal boundaries, converting thoughts and feelings into speech, knowing when to talk in a group, understanding how to resonate with the experiences and emotions of fellow addicts, and acknowledging the relevance of self-disclosure in a group setting. Staff need to know of these characteristics of ASD and must make appropriate accommodations.

The stress of group treatment and of staff not understanding ASD can lead to premature discharge from residential rehabilitation services. The person with an ASD may well become convinced that such services can never be effective. I would very much like to see rehabilitation services becoming more ASD friendly, and the development of an addiction treatment model specifically designed for those who have an ASD.

I have found that sometimes the person with an ASD can decide to end an addiction without therapeutic support. This takes great determination, and relies on one of the characteristics of ASD, namely that, once a decision has been made, the person is unwavering in seeking resolution and the desired outcome. However, the recommended treatment is conventional rehabilitation services and continuity of support.

Once the addiction is seemingly at an end, there is still the risk of relapse. It is important for the person with an ASD and their family members to accept lapses before there is complete and enduring freedom from addiction. It will be important that the person does not interact with previous drug or gaming associates, the associated culture and potential triggers. There will need to be support for stress and emotion management, encouragement to increase the network of social contacts and enjoyable social experiences, and the introduction of a new life style and schedule of daily activities. There will also need to be consideration of harm reduction and controlled usage versus total abstinence. Recovering from addiction is a long road, but the journey and destination may be life-saving.

This book is an important review of the issues associated with addiction and ASD. It will provide encouragement for parents to take action, and for professionals working the area of ASD to screen for addiction, and then to modify their treatment for addiction to accommodate the characteristics of ASD.

ACKNOWLEDGEMENTS

There are many people who helped to make this book a reality. We want to thank our colleagues within the substance use and addiction field: Kay Atchison, Katie Cooper, Claire Seibert, Charise Caruth-Iacono, Morris Godwin, Neida Rodrigues, and the amazing Techs, PAs, and Nurses of UNC WakeBrook who offered much needed help, advice, and patience. Special thanks go to Michael Wieleba who generously provided support as well as innumerable insights, and Dr. Joseph Williams for offering exceptional close readings of the more challenging journal articles.

We also want to thank our friends and colleagues from the autism world who shared their experiences, offered advice, read chapters, edited surveys, and provided support for this book: Mary van Bourgondien, Laura Klinger, Rob Christian, and members of the NC Autism Alliance, Laurie Nederveen, Renee Clark, Hunter Blanton, Alex Griffin, Kate Hall, Cathy Pratt, and Jayson Delisle. Special thanks to Mike Chapman and Glenna Osborne from the UNC TEACCH Autism Program for allowing us to pick your brains and benefit from all your knowledge.

Thanks also to the wonderful professionals who work with college students with autism across the country, who shared their experiences and creative strategies to help students: Marc Ellison (Marshall University), Gerard D. Hoefling (Drexel University), Sue Kabot (Nova Southeastern University), DeAnn Lechtenberger (Texas Tech University), Mitchell Nagler (Adelphi University), and Vannee Cao-Nguyen (University of West Florida). Thank you Brent Wilson from Aspies Central, Emily Marchetta from SoberRecovery, and Mike from Shroomery.org for allowing us to include comments from your amazing website forums.

Thank you Nick Halpern for your research and editing.

We want to especially thank our friend Dave Spicer, who was willing to share his most personal thoughts and experiences, helping us to understand and appreciate the challenges of living with autism and substance use issues. You are an inspiration to us and many others. Thank you.

Of course, this book would never have existed without the support and patience of our families. Thanks for sharing us with this project over the last year, and for putting up with our absences and distractions. We couldn't have done this without you.

INTRODUCTION

When we first decided to address this topic and eagerly shared it with others, the response, for the most part, was bewilderment or indifference. We began to wonder if this quest was relevant. Would it lead us to a rare anomaly or something altogether mythical? Was each case of autism and addiction no different than a sighting of a giant ibis or a unicorn? After many searches of the internet with words like *addiction, autism* or *heroin and Asperger's* or *Ecstasy and Autism* we realized that what we were investigating was there in plain sight, all over the web, with hundreds of postings and comments from people with an autism diagnosis struggling with a substance use diagnosis (SUD). Not only were their forums and chatrooms full of participants reaching out to one another for understanding and help and receiving support and validation, but there were also addiction treatment centers dedicating lengthy and detailed webpages to descriptions of tailored treatments for individuals with an autism spectrum diagnosis (ASD).

But the forum and chat posts of Tweakster, Koolboy and Leavemealone, or the targeted advertising tactics of treatment centers to lure individuals with an ASD into rehab did not offer enough legitimate evidence to warrant a book. We sought research and journal articles to back up what the internet had yielded, but the current literature on the topic was sparse. There appeared to be few research studies addressing the intersection of autism spectrum and substance use diagnoses, and most of those we found concluded that the risk of an SUD was lower for those with an ASD compared to the general population.

We were surprised by how few articles there were, especially compared to studies addressing the relationships between autism or substance dependence and other mental health diagnoses such as depression, anxiety, attention deficit hyperactivity disorder (ADHD), or an intellectually challenged diagnosis (ICD). This was another red flag for us, given that many adolescents and adults with an autism diagnosis often have additional diagnoses that are usually associated with SUD. Anxiety, depression, ADHD, and ICD are risk factors for developing substance abuse. Adults and adolescents with autism have higher rates of anxiety, depression, ADHD, and ICD than the general population. Remembering our middle school math, we wondered why no one had applied the transitive property to autism and substance use diagnoses. If A=B and B=C then A=C, it would stand to reason that adolescents and adults with an autism diagnosis would be at risk of developing an addiction. Yet there didn't seem to be any evidence, and as anyone in the medical field knows, speculation is fine, but evidence is a required component.

But we did have evidence, albeit anecdotal and intuitive. We had the postings, we had treatment facilities, we had some qualitative studies, some case studies, and one related quantitative study, there was a book addressing alcohol and Asperger's (Tinsley and Hendrickx 2008), and we had found a number of commonalities and connections between the two diagnoses. For instance, when we saw this quote, "It was all very confusing. I remember isolating on the playground, watching all the other children laughing and playing and smiling, and not feeling like I could relate at all. I felt different. I didn't feel as if I were one of them. Somehow, I thought, I didn't fit in" (AA 2002, p.281), we speculated that it could easily be attributed to someone with an autism diagnosis looking back at their childhood, even though it came straight from *Alcoholics Anonymous: The Big Book*. As we did our research, we not only felt that we had more than enough material for a book; we felt that drug and alcohol misuse and dependence among those with an autism diagnosis was indeed prevalent, and it was imperative that it be addressed.

We are not disconnected from this topic; we have relationships to both diagnoses, personally and professionally. And though we may not have witnessed the intersection up close, we felt confident there was a connection. Since our early and informal investigation of substance use within the autism community was initially met with puzzlement, it was clear that broader and more targeted outreach was necessary.

We crafted three surveys: one directed to professionals working with individuals with an ASD, one for self-advocates (that is, an individual with an ASD), and one for the family members or loved ones of an individual with an ASD. We sent these surveys out to various agencies, college programs, vocational service providers, professional societies, support groups, and several personal and professional mailing lists. The professionals' survey was short, just three open-ended questions asking how often the respondent encountered clients with both an autism and substance use diagnosis, a brief assessment of particular clients—the drug(s) of choice and their circumstances—and then a follow-up regarding the choice of intervention(s).

The self-advocate and family surveys varied in length depending on how the questions were answered, so that individuals could skip large sections that weren't relevant to their experiences with drugs or alcohol. These surveys had questions like: "At what age did you or your family member first consume alcoholic beverages?" or "Has another relative, friend, doctor, or other healthcare worker ever told you/your family member with an ASD that they were concerned about your/their drinking?" The replies we received from these surveys were invaluable. Particular responses are quoted throughout the book, including some answers from those in the autism community who reported no personal connection to substance abuse.

Still, although surveys are helpful, having a back-and-forth with individuals via email conversations or, even better, in person, is invaluable. Several people in the field of autism support as well as self-advocates spoke with us and offered their expertise and understanding. The experiences and creativity they shared add both practicality and intimacy to this book. We hope family members, loved ones, and self-advocates, the ultimate authorities when it comes to ASD and/or SUD diagnoses, can benefit from the information offered by these and other professionals, self-advocates, and family members, as well as from comments and insights that we plucked from websites, blogs, and forums.[1]

Our book begins with brief overviews of autism spectrum and substance use diagnoses, commonly referred to by the DSM-5 (APA 2013) as "autism spectrum disorder" and "substance use disorder." Because the word *disorder*, though commonly used in association with

---

[1]   Readers should note that quotes taken from blogs, forums and the comments sections of various internet sites have been quoted directly, retaining the original spelling and grammar of their authors..

a variety of mental health and developmental diagnoses, could be interpreted as stigmatizing, we opted for *diagnosis* instead. Much of the autism community does not view its neuroatypical way of thinking as disordered, nor does it consider some of the concurrent symptoms such as sensory sensitivities or repetitive behaviors as a significant liability. As the author of *Pretending to Be Normal: Living with Asperger's Syndrome*, Liane Holliday Willey advised, "We are not broken; we are otherwise fixed as wonderfully unique thinkers" (quoted in Attwood, Evans, and Lesko 2014, p.323).

The substance abuse community is different; though there are activists and advocates who argue for destigmatization, harm reduction, and treatment options, there appears to be no groundswell movement celebrating pride in their differences. Even SUD support groups tout anonymity as a form of protection, and this can be seen as propagating stigma, a fear of being "outed" rather than pride. The discrepancy makes sense if we look at how both diagnoses develop.

Since autism is most often diagnosed at an early age, families, loved ones, and professionals swoop in to support the innocent toddler or preschooler who may be out of sync with their peers. Substance dependence often begins in early adolescence and develops slowly among its unwitting users. Teens or adults initially reach for substances to deal with trauma, pain, or just as a means to fit in, to seem "cool." By the time someone is hooked, their sickness may have led to poor choices and actions that result in alienating their supports. It is more likely family and community members would have an easier time rallying behind a sweet—even when tantrumming—child than a moody, unkempt, and seemingly dishonest teen, but this does not mean that one condition deserves more compassion than another. This is why the majority of the time we deliberately omit "disorder" with both diagnoses.

Though the authors of the DSM-5 decided to omit the word *addiction* because it can be stigmatizing, throughout this book we use several words to indicate substance use disorder such as addiction, dependence, and abuse. Acknowledging word choice is important. Just as the autism community stopped using "an autistic" as a noun to describe a person with an autism diagnosis, so an individual affected by an SUD does not like to be referred to by others as "an addict." Of course, there are nuances in naming, and often words once considered offensive can be re-appropriated by a marginalized group. Just as the long-reviled word *queer*, once assigned to members of the LGBT community, has now been re-appropriated by many in that community as an accurate term for those on the sexual spectrum who do not wish to be labeled or categorized, many with an ASD now proudly refer to themselves as "Autistics." Of course, one's relationship to the power of language can be questioned. Using "autistic" as a noun currently feels like an "in-group term" that could be offensive if used by someone who may not identify as having an ASD. In AA/Narcotics Anonymous (NA) meetings, one introduces oneself by one's first name followed by, *and I am an addict.* Ownership of the term is important, but in writing this book, we are looking at both autism spectrum and substance use diagnoses from the outside, and do not therefore use *autistic* or *addict* as a noun.

We must admit that we generalize about both diagnoses. Of course, there are commonalities with both, and there are also many differences. For instance, an addiction to alcohol presents differently from an addiction to cocaine. The drug of choice has a significant impact on behaviors, treatment, and outcomes. With an autism spectrum diagnosis the word *spectrum* makes sense since there is definitely a range among those diagnosed. Almost half of those diagnosed with autism have co-occurring intellectual challenges (CDC 2016). In this book, we do not make a distinction between those with autism who do or do not have an intellectually challenged diagnosis (ICD). The studies we reference do make a distinction; most of the studies regarding autism and substance use imply that the participants do not have a co-occurring ICD. There are also studies cited in this book that address individuals with an ICD with no mention of an ASD.

As with autism, there is not a great deal of empirical evidence regarding the rates of an SUD among the intellectually challenged, but research suggests that though overall substance use is low among those with intellectual challenges, substance abuse is high (Chapman and Wu 2012). In the past, many examples in this book, such as independent living, post-secondary education, marriages and partnerships, and work–life balance may have only seemed relevant to individuals with an ASD without an ICD, but that assumption wouldn't be accurate. Individuals with an ICD can certainly embark on all of these traditional, adult rites of passage.

This book is not geared toward one end of the spectrum or the other—it is targeting those affected by an autism spectrum diagnosis who may also have a co-occurring substance use diagnosis. Even though autism is associated with very particular components such as impaired social functioning or heightened sensory sensitivities, its manifestation in individuals offers an array of different presentations. Given an ASD presents in both predictable and wholly unpredictable ways, we anticipate this book's audience will cherry pick from these chapters what is relevant to them.

This book also doesn't make many distinctions regarding socio-economic status, race, cultural differences, gender identification, and a host of other distinguishing factors that impact each individual and their supports (or lack thereof). There is no need to cite evidence-based studies to assert that those with the financial means receive better care and treatment that improve outcomes. There may be outliers that politicians can point to, but having the financial ability to pick and choose particular treatment modalities allows for significantly different outcomes from not having options. Where one resides, what schools one may attend, how much time one's loved ones can offer one, simply put, having choices, offers the opportunity for successful outcomes.

When those with the financial resources judge the "choices" of those without means, for instance, accusing a parent of purchasing a cell phone instead of paying for treatment or refusing treatment options due to their location, this illustrates the fundamental misunderstanding that people without the means have as much flexibility as those who have money. Treatment may be too costly and/or inconvenient and may require time that an individual's inflexible employer will not allow. Choosing a cell phone and perhaps downloading helpful treatment apps and maintaining regular contact with their loved ones when they are working more than one job may be the best and only option they have.

We have both worked for institutions that provide quality ASD or SUD treatment to those without the means, and we are grateful that they exist. But we both know that these institutions are always in flux, depending on grants and awards, government distributions, and other financial resources to prop them up. We have witnessed waitlists for diagnostics and treatment that may be as long as a year. We have seen first hand how frustrating the system can be for those who do not have the wherewithal to navigate it. We have also seen other inequalities. For example, while researching this book there was a study that showed that even though autism is equally prevalent among all races, white children are more likely to receive an autism diagnosis than

African-American or Latino children (who are either misdiagnosed with ADHD or other mental health diagnoses, or simply assumed to have a behavior problem) (Mandell *et al.* 2007). These examples are a minute illustration of the huge health disparities that exist among different groups, and must be acknowledged.

It is our hope that the audience for this book constitutes a spectrum as well. Autism and substance abuse specialists offered their expertise as we wrote this book, and we hope that professionals in both fields will benefit from what was shared. This book illustrates how both diagnoses impact one another. We follow up with advice on how to screen, treat, and educate individuals impacted by either diagnoses. We hope that educators, vocational coaches, disabilities service providers, and the range of service providers who may find themselves working with adolescents or adults with an autism or substance use diagnosis will turn to this book when necessary. We also believe that this book is critical to self-advocates questioning their current diagnoses. The book is also written for the family and loved ones of those who have one diagnosis and suspect the other. When we were visiting our local Autism Society's bookstore and picked up a book about autism and the law, one of the bookstore's staff wistfully remarked: "That is a book the autism community should read before they have legal troubles—to avoid them—but unfortunately they usually get it after" (Kate Hall, personal communication, March 29, 2017). For the autism community, we hope this book has a preventative component and can help to protect against the development of an SUD.

As we mention throughout this book, there is little evidence-based information regarding those dually diagnosed with an ASD and SUD. Well after we considered much of the research phase of this book complete and started writing, a director from one of the University of North Carolina's (UNC) TEACCH (Treatment and Education of Autistic and related Communication Handicapped Children) Autism Program Centers sent us a newly released population-based study of over 26,900 individuals with an ASD that documented an increased risk of substance use-related problems among the ASD population when compared to the general population (Butwicka *et al.* 2017). This was the first quantitative research that substantiated what we had already suspected. The validation was both helpful and frustrating, since confirmation of an official comorbidity between an SUD and

ASD is quite new, so it may be a while before treatment modalities for this dual diagnosis are studied and proven effective.

But evidence-based research, particularly with the outcomes of something like SUD treatment, where the goal is to maintain productivity, health, and a good quality of life, are sometimes hard to measure. This book offers particular treatment options that may work for some individuals with autism and substance dependence diagnoses and not others. Since neither diagnosis has a cure, the goal is to achieve the best possible outcomes. For some, it may be harm reduction, that is, to lessen substance use without insisting on total abstinence. For others, such a goal would be unfeasible, and their treatment would require total abstinence in order to lead the best quality of life.

We also had to remind ourselves that sometimes the non-stop rallying cry for evidence-based medicine in social sciences like psychology might be misguided. Unlike medicine, where healing a bone or shrinking a tumor offers empirical results, the subjectivity of determining quality of life is often messier. Not everything can be measured numerically or exactly. The current trend for fields like psychology to emulate models established in the hard sciences would lead us to believe that volatile variables such as feelings, thoughts, or moods can be accounted for precisely. We know first hand that studies can be biased and may reflect predispositions or misconceptions brought to the study by the researchers—such as those studies we encountered citing the core features of autism as protective factors against developing a substance use diagnosis. This is to say, we endorse certain screenings, treatments, and educational options that seem viable for those with an ASD grappling with an SUD, but have no official proof they will be effective. We highly advocate that everyone involved view any treatment options with trust tempered with skepticism.

Genetic science is currently looked to as offering irrefutable evidence as well as possible treatment. Neuroscience may reduce or eliminate the speculative trial-and-error approach in psychological and psycho-educational treatments. We touch on both these topics because they are in the vanguard of research methodology. There is a vast and complicated array of research in the area of autism and addiction, and we explore and report on studies where there is some overlap. We hope that the experts in these fields will continue to share their findings, since they promise to offer innovative diagnostic and treatment options. On the other hand, we would be remiss if we did not mention there are mental health and disability activists who fervently argue against this sort of research, implying there is some sort of perfect genome or "normal" brain function. It is important to pause and contemplate their position, since genetic and neuroscientific research propagating "normality" as a goal further marginalizes and creates additional self-doubt and helplessness for those outside of what constitutes the definition of "normal" (Solomon 2012).

Taking a step back from evidence-based approaches can sometimes offer room to innovate. Though there are currently no officially sanctioned treatment options, there are many acceptable assessments and screening tools for both an ASD and SUD. This book is an investigation, not a manual. We offer knowledge, strategies, and suggestions that should work well in specific contexts such as an addiction and detox unit or a college program tailored for individuals with an ASD. It is our intention to offer appropriate tools for individuals in either the ASD or SUD field to begin the process of getting proper assistance. Often there is a patient who fits a particular protocol and there are others who don't. For instance, on detox units after a patient has withdrawn from the substance of choice, the symptoms they may have been masking or treating usually emerge, or traits that should diminish remain or even intensify. This account of one individual who did not know he had an autism diagnosis when he was treated for his alcohol dependence is an example:

> ...because all of the denial, all of the rationalization, all of the blaming, the whole—pardon me—shit-storm that is active addiction precludes figuring out what's actually going on underneath. And I mean selfishness, self-centeredness that's the *core of our disease, is the core of our malady* it says in the AA big book. The average alcoholic, self-centered to the extreme isn't going to do this or that or the other thing and here I am with a neurological condition named for self-centeredness—*autos*—the self, and you pour alcohol on top of that which tends to induce more self-centered behavior, so of course it's going to go that way. So what you think of is you stop drinking, you remove the alcohol and start working on the "ism" and practice these steps and all of that stuff and then the tendency toward self-centeredness will lift and you'll regain the sense of connection with other people that you had before and all of that stuff, and I'm like, you know, I never had that. There's still something missing. There's still something that isn't right. (Anonymous, personal communication, October 15, 2017)

For families and those working with adults and adolescents with an autism diagnosis we hope to debunk the myth that autism's core features reduce the risk of substance abuse. Given the low rates of SUD screening in medical settings in general, increasing awareness of the risks, prevalence, and impact of a substance use diagnosis is critical.

Although this book addresses both autism and substance use diagnoses sometimes interchangeably, both diagnoses fall under that broad category—mental health—and are often misunderstood, underdiagnosed, and undertreated. The distinctions are addressed, but the most important difference, that SUD can be deadly, must be emphasized, particularly given the current opioid crisis. We feel compelled to dispel the stereotypes in order to raise awareness.

> The day that Barbara and Brian Goldner lost their son began with triumph. Brandon, 23, had recently started a new job as a retail clerk, and he texted a photo of his pay stub to his dad...
>
> "He was so proud," Brian says.
>
> The day before, Barbara and Brandon had grocery-shopped, as the two customarily did... Barbara drove Brandon back to his apartment, near where his parents lived. Brandon had Asperger syndrome, an autism spectrum disorder, and his parents were pushing him toward independence. Having a place of his own, like having a job, was significant progress. The mother and son talked. Then they said goodbye, and Barbara left.
>
> The "incredibly sweet" Brandon was also "incredibly smart, incredibly well versed about politics," his father says. "Very much a thinker," says Brian. "He had a strong desire to be successful. It was a challenge for him to hold down a job—but he had a job."
>
> And yes, he could be "gullible," as his mother describes him, "innocent" in a certain sense. Asperger's can have that effect.
>
> These things and many more, the Goldners knew about their child.
>
> What they did not know was that Brandon had started using heroin.
>
> ...Nor did they know that Brandon had been taken to Rhode Island Hospital's emergency room after accidentally overdosing and being revived by emergency responders seven times in the previous two months—including three times in one six-day period. (Miller 2016)

It may be hard to reconcile the use of the words *gullible* and *innocent* as descriptors of someone with a heroin addiction, but they are accurate. No one is immune to this crisis or the other well-known risks associated with alcohol and drug use. If this book does nothing else than to raise awareness, to recommend parents and providers of adolescents and adults with an ASD not to make assumptions, and regularly, in a non-judgmental manner, to check in and ask about drug and alcohol use, then it is a success. Of course, this check in should probably be done with the majority of adolescents and young adults. It may not prevent drug addiction or overdoses, but it can reduce the risk and perhaps the stigma that prevents individuals from reaching out, and family members and providers from asking. In the introduction to *Far from the Tree: Parents, Children and the Search for Identity* (2012, p.26), an extraordinary book addressing difference, Andrew Solomon notes: "A tolerant society softens parents and facilitates self-esteem, but that tolerance has evolved because individuals with good self-esteem have exposed the flawed nature of prejudice." As professionals, researchers, and parents, this project helped us to reassess our own prejudices that have affected our tolerance. We hope we can pass on what we have learned, and offer assistance and hope to others.

CHAPTER 1

AUTISM AND SUBSTANCE ABUSE AND ADDICTION
A Brief Overview

AUTISM OVERVIEW

The current rates of autism spectrum diagnoses in the US are estimated to be somewhere around 1 in 68. It is well known that an ASD, like a substance use diagnosis, favors males, with boys 4.5 times more likely to be diagnosed with an ASD than girls (CDC 2016). The worldwide prevalence of autism is said to be about 1 percent (Autism Society 2015b). Given that 30 years ago the incidence of autism was about 1 in 2000, there have been a number of theories and explanations for the steep increase. One explanation is that autism may have been misdiagnosed in the past, at least until the 1970s and 1980s, when the diagnostic criteria for autism expanded significantly. Before this change, those with an ASD who were more able were often misdiagnosed with other mental health conditions or not diagnosed at all, and those with intellectual challenges were diagnosed as having mental retardation, not autism. Greater awareness and understanding of the signs and symptoms of an ASD led to more individuals being diagnosed. The age of diagnosis is also getting younger and younger. Recent studies indicate that infants can now be diagnosed via MRI (magnetic resonance imaging scan). A new study has found that a brain scan of infants with siblings who had an autism diagnosis identified aspects of brain development that accurately predict development of an autism spectrum diagnosis (Callaway 2017).

What determines if someone has an autism diagnosis? The three main categories of development that are affected by an autism diagnosis are communication, social skills, and unusual interests and behaviors (CDC 2015). Some of the famous red flags associated with autism in a child are:

- Not responding to their name by the time the child turns one.

- Minimal or no eye contact and a desire to be alone.

- Not pointing at objects or responding to an object that is pointed to by another.

- Finding small and unexpected changes to routine unusually distressing.

- Having a delay in speech or in language skill.

- Having unusual reactions to sights, smells, tastes, sounds and texture or touch (sensory issues).

(CDC 2015)

Experts believe that a major contributing factor to the increase of the incidence of autism diagnoses is the broadening of the definition of autism spectrum disorder to include those individuals with less impairment and normal to above-average IQs. Asperger's Syndrome (AS) was introduced in 1994. Asperger's remained a separate subtypeof autism until recently, when it was folded into the single diagnosis of ASD. Like those with autism, individuals with AS have difficulty with social interactions and have a restricted range of interests and/or repetitive behaviors. Unlike those with an autism diagnosis, individuals with AS do not have significant delays or difficulties in language or impaired cognitive development (Autism Speaks 2017a). The *Diagnostic and Statistical Manual of Mental Disorders*, Fourth Edition (DSM-IV-TR), the American Psychiatric Association's diagnostic manual, had autistic disorder and Asperger's disorder as two distinct diagnoses (APA 2000). The recent update of this manual, the DSM-5, offered one umbrella diagnosis—autism spectrum disorder—which not only added Asperger's to the autism diagnosis, but also pervasive developmental disorder—not otherwise specified, better known as PDD-NOS (APA 2013). PDD-NOS is a diagnosis where there are some but not all of the deficits that determine an autism diagnosis: social, communication, or behaviors and interests (usually the first two are represented, while the repetitive behaviors and special interests are less prevalent) (Yale Child Study Center 2013). The expanded definition of an ASD to include these two "higher functioning" diagnoses was met with mixed responses. Many families of children diagnosed with AS as well as AS self-advocates do not like being reassigned a different diagnostic label, and fervently cling to their Asperger's or "Aspie" identity (Rosin 2014). Those who embrace the autism moniker suspect the Asperger's community's desire to remain separate from the autism community as buying into a false hierarchy—not unlike someone addicted to alcohol feeling superior to someone injecting heroin. Those who work in autism services felt that the single umbrella might, in the long run, be useful in that in some states, if a child received the diagnosis of Asperger's or PDD-NOS, it was difficult to get services, whereas an autism diagnosis guaranteed support. In this book, ASD is used as a catch-all, even though some of the individuals or books quoted may refer to Asperger's or PDD-NOS.

According to the Asperger/Autism Network (AANE), some professionals currently suspect that as many as 1 in every 250 people has an Asperger's profile (AANE 2017). A recent study in England estimated the prevalence of AS closer to 1 in every 100 (Brugha *et al.* 2011). The reason it is important to hone in on Asperger's for this book is that (a) studies tend to focus on this diagnosis, possibly because those with an AS diagnosis might be more verbally adept and able to offer qualitative data about themselves, and (b) it appears that a number of adults with an AS diagnosis who suffer from a substance use diagnosis were either misdiagnosed with psychiatric, behavioral, or emotional problems, or were just considered "odd" or "quirky" and turned to drugs or alcohol as either a means to fit in, self-medicate, or cope. Given the high numbers of adults recently diagnosed and the many who may remain undiagnosed, AANE believes a significant number of people from past generations with Asperger's profiles have slipped through many Asperger's/autism diagnostic nets (AANE 2017). It is possible that many of these undiagnosed adults may be currently abusing substances, in treatment, in recovery, or in some cases, in the criminal justice system (King and Murphy 2014).

Many of the examples cited for this book are primarily focused on the experiences of those with an ASD who are predominantly in mainstream settings: school, employment, and in the community. It is unclear if these individuals had exposure to drugs and alcohol because they were connected to the community, or if the stress of being connected to the community was the impetus for alcohol and drug use. Many appear to be struggling to "fit in" with their non-autistic peers, and it isn't clear if individuals may turn to drinking and drugs because substance use is what everyone does when they socialize, or if drugs and/or alcohol use eases social deficits and facilitates socializing. Either way, substance use can be seen as a coping strategy.

When broaching the topic for this book with many in the autism community, the reaction was either indifference or cognitive dissonance—either way, the implication was that these two diagnoses had no relationship to one another, and making connections between them was often dismissed and treated as something akin to science fiction. Those we reached out to held up many of the social and sensory aspects of autism as protective factors, shielding the individual with an ASD from the "harmful influences" of the neurotypical (NT) world. Sensory challenges such as picky eating, limited diets, skin and olfactory sensitivities may discourage an individual with an autism diagnosis from ingesting, snorting, or injecting a mind-altering substance. Sensitivities to noise levels and avoidance of loud environments such as bars or parties may protect individuals with an ASD from joining these raucous gatherings. The social aspect of substance use was another protective factor—attending social events, participating in groups, or developing friendships may all be a struggle for someone with autism, and they therefore might opt out of the typical adolescent or young adult social scene. A smaller circle of friends or relationships might limit individuals with an ASD from gaining access to recreational drugs and minimize opportunities to join in activities where alcohol or drugs may be readily available, like frat parties or clubbing. Another protective factor cited is the rule-bound nature of many individuals with an ASD. Rules bring comfort by providing guidance and structure to what can be a very confusing world. Many with an ASD feel a strong need to follow the rule of law and may not understand or tolerate the illicit behaviors of others. Buying and experimenting with illegal drugs or drinking when underage may be too much of a provocation and disruption for an individual with an ASD. Also, seeking out and buying illegal drugs on the street would be a challenge for people with limited social skills and a deterrent for those with a strong rule-bound nature (Ramos *et al.* 2013).

These perceived protective factors may not be as relevant today as they were in the past. As mentioned previously, individuals with autism are being diagnosed at an earlier age, and therefore more young children are receiving treatment and interventions. Offering early interventions and continuing treatment into adolescence can improve many of the deficits that may have previously been perceived as protective factors. More strategies to prevent sensory challenges, better social skills, and improved flexibility around routines and rules can open up the world of the individual with an ASD, but can also expose them to more risks. Improved outcomes for individuals with an ASD mean more opportunities for inclusion in mainstream life with non-autistic peers in education, work, and in the community. And more opportunities may include opportunities to join their peers who are enjoying drugs and alcohol. More opportunities can also mean added stressors that might lead someone with an autism diagnosis to seek alcohol or drugs for relief. More opportunities could also lead to more easily accessing illegal drugs, as explained, for example, in this post from a blogger with an ASD:

> ...opiates and me get on a bit too well. Thankfully I've never been physically addicted, but good grief I could take opiates till the cows came home. Or didn't. Or whatever. I wouldn't care. Cows? What cows?
>
> At the peak of my opiate encounter, I was using heroin every second day more or less for about two years, plus all the other things I was using on top of or alongside it. (Aspiehepcat July 26, 2012)

For many students with an ASD, the schools and often families aim for inclusion in classes with neurotypical students, particularly if they have average or above-average academic skills. "Mainstreaming" is financially beneficial to schools that have to shoulder the monetary burden of implementing the US Individuals with Disabilities Education Act (IDEA), a piece of legislation that is supposed to ensure that students with disabilities are offered the same quality of public education as their NT peers. This legislation is a huge gain for the differently-abled and their families, but unfortunately for the public schools in certain districts, the funds are minimal to cover the extensive costs of educating those with documented disabilities. With residents demanding lower taxes and, at the same time, with school districts mandated to offer quality education for all, the smaller self-contained classes, or classes only including exceptional students with special needs, are fewer in US public schools than in the past. "From 2004 through 2013, the percentage of students ages 6 through 21 served under IDEA, Part B, educated inside the regular class 80% or more of the day increased from 51.8 percent to 62.1 percent" (US Department of Education 2015, p.xxvi). Some see this as a victory of inclusion; others see it as a loss of focus on particular students' needs. If the rise in rates of autism in the last ten years is factored in, the result is a growing number of students with an autism diagnosis spending most of their school day in regular education classrooms alongside their typically-developing peers. This can bring with it many benefits and challenges. Students may struggle academically and, of course, socially (given social deficits can be a major component of autism), leaving many struggling to fit in any way they know how:

> I will admit I have Asperger's, and I could tell you it ain't easy at all. I have been sober 13 months off of heroin. One of the reasons why I turned to alcohol and drugs was because I felt unaccepted from peers through my school years. I have through my life had trouble getting a girlfriend. I could make great conversations but I always felt different from everybody. I still struggle with this issue. (SoberRecovery Forums August 19, 2011)

Most parents worry about their child's exposure to negative influences, undesirable behaviors, and peer pressure during the school years, but this can be especially concerning to parents of students with an ASD in the mainstream setting. The combination of seeking acceptance via peer relationships combined with challenged executive functioning and possibly compromised choice-making skills can magnify parental concerns for the safety of that student. Parents of adolescents with an ASD are not immune from the worries of teen drug use:

> My 17-year-old son has just recently been diagnosed with Asperger's syndrome. After several really rough years of being bullied and having difficulty with maintaining friendships, we began to see him drifting towards "the wrong crowd" and using marijuana. At first, we assumed it was an experimental thing, but has since caused him to be arrested for possession. He continued to use despite mandatory drug testing. (Hutten 2010)

More inclusion of students with an autism spectrum diagnosis during the primary and secondary school years has led to more inclusion for these students in college settings. There are no clear statistics on college enrolment of students with autism, but it is estimated that they comprise anywhere from 0.7 to 1.9 percent of the college population. These numbers are likely to increase exponentially in the coming years, and will continue to force post-secondary academic institutions to expand their understanding of individuals with an ASD in order to accommodate the increase of students with a diagnosis (VanBergeijk, Klin, and Volkmar 2008). The availability of community colleges and online college programs, as well as the many college programs designed for supporting students with learning differences, has expanded the possible options for a college experience for students with an ASD. Universities and colleges are offering more supports for students with an ASD as they are gaining more experience working with these students, and understanding their needs in the college setting. The Americans with Disabilities Act (ADA) requires colleges to provide "reasonable accommodations" for their differently-abled students (ADA National Network 2017); however, supports through the disability services offices on college campuses typically address academic success by mandating professors to modify their classrooms, curriculum, or requirements in order to level the playing field for students with challenges. But these disability services often cannot adequately support the many needs that students may have in their daily life outside of the classroom (Palmer 2006).

The social aspect of a college experience—developing friendships, dating, living in a residential setting with other students—can be the most challenging aspect of college life for students with an ASD. The daily life skills required to be successful in the college setting, such as setting an alarm clock, getting to class on time, managing free time, taking care of personal hygiene, etc., are also not typically supported through the disability services offered at universities. There are often few, if any, supports available to address these issues (Palmer 2006). In a 2015 study of college students with an ASD, participants reported receiving extensive academic supports that helped with their academic success, but reported difficulties receiving support in the social and emotional domains (Gelbar, Shefcyk, and Reichow 2015). For many students, the only assistance they receive for these challenges comes from parents or family members or a counselor or "college coach" who may be hired by the family to provide supplemental support. Often students must navigate these challenging aspects of college life independently. This may account for the dismal statistics regarding high school and post-secondary graduation rates among students with an ASD: "Rates of post-secondary educational participation for youth with an ASD are substantially lower than the general population, with previous studies indicating 40% or fewer ever attend college and very few receive a degree" (Shattuck *et al.* 2012, p.1043).

With the better prognosis for students with an ASD who receive intensive and earlier intervention, we see more adults on the spectrum looking for competitive employment. However, employment rates are much lower for adults with an ASD as compared to adults without disabilities or with disabilities other than autism. In an article in the *Journal of the American Academy of Child and Adolescent Psychiatry* in 2013, Roux and her team report that young adults with autism spectrum diagnoses have worse employment outcomes in the first few years after high school than peers who are neurotypical or who have other types of disabilities. The study also found that the pay for the small numbers of those with autism who were working was significantly lower compared to young adults with other types of disabilities (Roux *et al.* 2013). Anecdotally, when individuals struggling with a substance use diagnosis were asked what triggers cravings, "boredom" was the most common answer (Elizabeth Kunreuther, personal communication, April 6, 2017). The boredom that could result from being underemployed or unemployed or not having access to proper recreational services could be a serious risk factor for adolescents and adults with an ASD to develop addictions. Certainly this is already evident regarding individuals with an autism diagnosis developing gaming and internet addictions (MacMullin, Lunsky, and Weiss 2016). For those adults with an ASD who are employed, they will also find themselves dealing with the day-to-day stressors that come with working—handling the responsibilities of the job, taking instruction from supervisors, getting along with co-workers, dealing with office politics, getting to and from work, etc.—that could easily lead to substance abuse.

> I know that I would not have been able to keep the jobs that I have had in my life if I had not used alcohol to give me the tools to do so. Most people would say that drinking alcohol while working is unequivocally a bad thing, and that being sober makes you a much more effective employee. In my case, however, I firmly believe that I was only able to do the jobs, and also to put on the act

of normality through sublimating my real self, because of alcohol. (Tinsley and Hendrickx 2008, p.74)

Whether an adult with an ASD is employed or not, lack of support and the stress of managing an independent life can lead to unpromising outcomes:

> When I am with people I do not know or know well, I find it difficult to know what to do. I usually shift into "silent mode" and just watch. I recall one departmental party two years ago that occurred in the midst of a rainstorm. I observed everyone in the room and realized that every single person was engaged in conversation, except me. It turned out that state of affairs lasted almost the entire party. I did not know if I was intentionally being ignored or not, but I remained in the room until every single person had left. Then I went to the blackboard and drew a picture of a woman caught in the rainstorm. The picture seemed to express the discomfort and hurt that I felt and I left it there to be discovered by others. (Prince-Hughes 2002, pp.102–103)

With earlier and more intensive intervention, the hope is that more individuals with an ASD will be able to attend college, work jobs, and live independently (or with minimal support) in the community. The most common available option for many of these individuals, besides living with their parents indefinitely—which appears to be the trajectory for most adults with an ASD—is to live in the community with limited supports (Volkmar and Wolf 2013). With minimal federal and state dollars available for supported residential housing options, group homes, or supported living programs, families are finding it necessary to be creative in developing successful residential options. They may choose to build a basement apartment in their home or purchase a house in the community for their adult child or possibly partner with another family who also needs a residential option for their grown-up child. These options can be expensive if the family also has to pay for staff to come into the home and provide support as needed. Though many adults face intense stressors when trying to manage independently, an adult with an autism diagnosis may have additional challenges when dealing with financial responsibilities, home upkeep, getting along with neighbors, transportation, etc. With limited support, living in the community can be very nerve-wracking for the individual with an ASD:

> Every day I have to function in two different realities. There is my everyday reality. It is a world full of deadlines, schedules, and demands. It is loud and confusing. There are so many rules, and very few of them actually make any sense. Then there is my native reality. It is the place where everything comes easy. However, it is a place I only get to visit, to retreat to when I have no other demands or if the world gets to be so much that I just cannot take it anymore. The reality is I have to navigate the neurotypical world to provide for my children. I have to advocate for their needs. I had to obtain an education and get a job. I cannot walk out of my job because of social interactions. I have to live in the neurotypical world even if it is not my native world. (James 2016)

There is an assumption that due to compromised social functioning, individuals with autism prefer solitude. For some this may be true, but, just like the general population, adults with an ASD want relationships and many are partnering, having children, and dealing with the everyday stresses of family life. Maintaining a relationship and raising children is challenging for everyone, but can be especially challenging for those with an ASD:

> I learned to burp babies and grew adept with a diaper. And yet I know that I was not as responsive a father to little William, Robert, and John as I would have liked to be. Overwrought and preoccupied at home, I traveled whenever I could...just to find some solitude and calm myself down... (Page 2009, p.183)

With the many challenges that individuals with an ASD may face in a neurotypical world, the advent of the digital revolution may benefit those on the autism spectrum. People with an ASD can be quite comfortable around technology and often have superior computer skills. The advent of technology as a driving force in our society has made life a lot easier for many with an ASD to navigate. Communication via social media, texting, and computer chats offers an easier means to socially connect. Fewer face-to-face interactions and more communication via a keyboard may benefit those with social challenges or social anxiety. The rise of the technology industry can offer ASD individuals with innate high-tech skills more options for employment. These kinds of jobs can require fewer social skills and more opportunities to work independently, something many employees on the spectrum may prefer:

> Around the age of 14, I filled in for a graphic designer who was working for my father at that time, typing and checking spellings in a large manuscript... I stepped in and finished his job twice as fast, with half as many spelling mistakes as he would have done. My family saw this potential and got me my own computer, which was used for playing computer games for a few years...but before long I had installed demo versions of professional graphic design software and was helping my father with his design work. (quoted in Attwood et al. 2014, p.212)

Improved technology, easier access to information, and the ability to bond with others via the internet have also provided individuals with autism more ways to connect and to find support. Websites specific to Asperger's Syndrome or ASD, chatrooms, and other online support opportunities are plentiful. Feeling part of the ASD community can be helpful to someone who may feel isolated or who struggles to fit into the neurotypical world around them: "I love the autism world. I love escaping into my obsession. It is peaceful and easy. I do not have to work hard to interact with other individuals with autism. We speak the same language—the language of autism" (James 2016).

The recent advent of computer technology along with earlier interventions and better outcomes, and an increased awareness and advocacy around ASD, have led to these expanded opportunities for individuals on the autism spectrum. This is a good thing, of course, but with broad social inclusion, individuals with an ASD are no longer as protected from the risks of living in a complicated and challenging world. As mentioned in the beginning of this section, approximately 1.5 percent of the US population has an ASD. Approximately 8.5 percent of US individuals aged 12 and up have a substance use diagnosis (NIDA 2016). Odds are, and research indicates, that there is a significant overlap between the two. Social anxiety, workplace expectations, and stress at home can lead any individual to seek solace from substances now and then, but the extra challenges and barriers those on the spectrum might encounter may certainly increase the risk of substance abuse, and self-advocates, their loved ones, and professionals in ASD and SUD services need to keep these risks in mind moving forward.

SUBSTANCE USE AND ADDICTION OVERVIEW

What is substance use disorder? Is it the same as addiction? Or substance abuse? Or substance dependence? What defines an addiction? How is substance use disorder diagnosed? Are people with autism at risk? Substance use disorder (SUD) is the American Psychiatric Association's careful blending of various addiction diagnoses used in the past (APA 2013). SUDs are usually categorized into three criteria: mild, moderate, and severe. The substances included in the DSM-5 are: alcohol, caffeine, cannabis, hallucinogens, inhalants, opioids, sedatives, stimulants, and tobacco. An individual is diagnosed when their use of alcohol and/or drugs affects their ability to function effectively. This may mean impaired health or a significant impact on school, work, or home life (SAMHSA 2015). According to the DSM-5, a diagnosis of SUD involves drugs that activate the brain's reward system with such intensity that everyday activities are neglected. Another criterion for an SUD is evidence of impaired control, social impairment, and risky behaviors. This book looks at alcohol, prescription drug misuse, and illegal drug use in conjunction with autism. Particular items on the DSM-5's substance list may not be covered simply because there is too little literature available to explore a connection between substances such as caffeine or inhalants and autism.

It is important to clarify that SUDs should not be confused with substance-induced disorders that are psychological disorders that are the result of drug use and abuse. The focus of this book is addiction,[1] but it should be noted that there are other forms of substance abuse that can impair one's health and can lead to dangerous outcomes. Often dependence is seen as the most dangerous form of misuse of a substance, but this can be misleading. For example, in the most recent Office of the Surgeon General's report, 7.8 percent of Americans reported having a SUD but almost 25 percent reported binge drinking

---

1   Though many countries use the word *addiction* to describe problems that arise due to habitual or compulsive substance use, the DSM-5 consciously omitted *addiction* in a diagnostic context. The authors of the DSM-5 note that the definition of addiction is uncertain and the use of the word could lead to a "potentially negative connotation" (APA 2013).

in the past month (Office of the Surgeon General 2016). Binge drinking is not only a symptom of an SUD, but even if there is no physical or emotional dependence involved, it can be a step toward developing a substance use diagnosis:

> I find that if I am drunk I can talk too [sic] woman a hell of a lot better than when I'm sober... I really can not [sic] talk too woman when I'm sober. I have no idea what to say to them, and when I try they pretend to like me so I'll buy them drinks or they will just get annoyed and walk off. However when I'm drunk I can talk to woman, I don't know what alcohol dose [sic] too [sic] me but I know what to say I know when too [sic] say it I know the best distance too stand from them I know how to look at them I know when to smile at them I know how to get numbers and when too [sic] kiss them. (Keay 2017)

The most comprehensive and accepted cause of addiction is now an illness or disease model. But, like an autism spectrum diagnosis, there are a myriad of viable and suspect theories surrounding the causes and treatments of an SUD. Just like Bruno Bettelheim's destructive theory that autism was the result of poor mothering (Bettelheim 1967), suspected causes of addiction have been equally dubious and many, like debunked theories of the root of autism, still linger. The most common postulate that continues to haunt those with addictions is a moral model. Today, the debate of whether addiction should be treated as a sin or sickness still permeates our culture. The moral model of addiction, which states those with a strong will are able to accomplish abstinence and those who cannot maintain sobriety are weak and flawed, still dominate our culture's view of substance use. Despite the constant support by the Surgeon General, World Health Organization, medical, and psychiatric professional organizations of illness models of addiction, the moral model persists. This is disappointing, since addiction as an illness with genetic components has been accepted for thousands of years. For instance, Plutarch's remark that "one drunkard begets another" alludes to a genetic component to addiction, and Aristotle's non-judgmental observations of the cooption of free will in relation to addiction preface today's brain mapping models (Franzwa 1998).

It is said that E. M. Jellinick (whose résumé and reputation in the addiction community has recently been questioned), with the help of his wife's personal success via Alcoholics Anonymous, called for addiction to be viewed as a disease similar to cancer, diabetes, or heart disease—a combination of behavioral, biological, and environmental factors (Greenberg 2013). The disease model of addiction is currently endorsed by the American Medical Association and the American Society of Addiction Medicine, as well as by self-help organizations such as Alcoholics and Narcotics Anonymous (AA/NA). But the use of the word "disease," itself, becomes suspect. Asperger's Syndrome was once labeled by the American Psychiatric Association as a disease, and is now labeled a developmental disorder. The definition of a disease is, as Greenberg notes, "what doctors say it is" (Greenberg 2013). But this seemingly at-times indiscriminate labeling can have a positive impact offering to destigmatize those with an SUD and to increase financial resources for treatment and research as well as the social capital of understanding and even, to some extent, acceptance.

The roots of substance use, like those of autism, are elusive. There appears to be a genetic component suggesting that individuals have a genetic predisposition toward being vulnerable to addictions. Environmental factors such as trauma can either activate these genes or the trauma itself can lead individuals to depend on substances to bring them some sort of solace. One individual we met shared that after arriving at college in the 1960s, not knowing at that time he had autism and having been socially and emotionally challenged all his childhood, he felt completely at sea within the structureless academic and social world that was his college environment. He reported how he began to unravel socially and academically, and found solace in the small-town bars after class.

> I got in trouble with alcohol not within years or even months but within a matter of weeks when I first started drinking. Once I started I didn't want to stop because the effect was *boy this is different* and I sure as hell wanted different. I felt so isolated up there and apart and different from everybody. I was just lost so it was self-medication right from the very beginning. (Dave Spicer, personal interview, October 1, 2016)

A substance use always has that element of choice tethered to it. The moral model insists that addiction, no matter how severe, is a choice made by an individual to seek and use a substance for relief. Alcoholics and Narcotics Anonymous, though very effective in helping individuals maintain recovery, has a moral code at the heart of their makeup: the Twelve Steps. But many find that drinking and drug use are not moral issues but rather symptoms of an illness. As Szalavitz put it: "No mainstream treatment for bipolar disorder or OCD [obsessive compulsive disorder] demands submission to a Higher Power, nor is this recommended in schizophrenia—let alone in care for flu, stroke, or dementia" (2016, p.221). Choice is often seen as picking between good (not using substances) and bad (using substances). Choice can also be seen as opting between right and wrong, virtue and sin, strength and weakness, etc. Most Western societies have not strayed away from this model and indeed, AA/NA are effective for many with an SUD, and the principal of choice is deeply rooted within both programs. Certainly, the "war on drugs" and the recent press regarding the high rates of incarceration have brought the moral approach toward addiction to the fore. No one would think of jailing someone for having and acting on their illness. The moralistic component woven into substance use has added a disturbingly dishonorable element to a diagnosis that is complicated and, at times, messy.

Many individuals who suffer from addiction harbor such great shame regarding their use that they use more in order to squelch their embarrassment. In *Thirst*, James B. Nelson, who was addicted to alcohol, describes his feelings of shame in a way many people with autism might be able to relate to: "I can only cover it [shame] up, hide it, or find some escape. Because I see myself not good enough to be accepted and loved as I am and since I am convinced that others would judge and withdraw if they really knew me, I must bury the deeper, chaotic parts of myself from view" (Nelson 2004, p.134). Later, he shares: "Nevertheless, there is reason to understand addiction as a particularly shame-based phenomenon. Simply put, compulsive behavior typically stems from trying to voice shame" (p.135). This compulsive behavior may not be the same as the compulsive or repetitive behaviors of those with an ASD, but there may be some similarities.

> swim was diagnosed with asperger's, social anxiety, and depression when swim was 15 and was prescribed 20mg of lexapro for two years. swim fiddled around with weed in highschool but not too much. swim loved alcohol throughout highschool though because it dumbed him down and helped him sleep. But he got way too into alcohol, as he does with everything he enjoys, and started distilling moonshine in his basement at age 17. By the time he made it to his freshman year in college, he had just recently picked

up a weed habit, and within two weeks, he started buying half ounces every two days and selling. within a month of his freshman year (no prior drug use other than pot and alcohol) he tried just about every drug other than heroin, crack, and meth. sometime within the first semester he started growing mushrooms in his dorm room, and frequently experimenting with xanax, psilocybin and lsd. Shortly after second semester began, he got in trouble with his parents because the drug use was consuming him. It wasnt anywhere near addiction, but he was soooo interested in drugs, especially mushrooms, that it became noticable. He hates how he has no control over his obsession with things that interest him, and therefore he finds drugs somewhat dangerous. (Shroomery.org January 31, 2013)

Despite the fact that some patients have said that their shame and the punishment that can ensue from substance use have been deterrents for the most part, punishment for illegal drug use has been ineffective treatment. This is not to say that punishing the behaviors of individuals while under the influence, such as criminalizing drunk driving, is not necessary, especially if the individual receives effective and compassionate treatment as part of their sentence (Yu, Evans, and Clark 2006). But punishment without treatment appears to be ineffective. It seems as though punishing individuals who have an SUD is akin to punishing a child with an ASD who has self-harming behaviors; such punishment can seem futile or counterproductive.

For those in the substance abuse field, there are the famous experiments of caged rats overdosing versus the happy rats' abstinence in Rat Park. In the 1970s, rats were isolated in a cage and offered water and water laced with heroin. The rats usually chose the latter and drank until they overdosed and died. Robert Alexander decided to try the same experiment, but instead of isolating the rats in stark cages, he built a complex for rats that had fun activities, lots of good food, a feeling of freedom, and most important, other rats. Alexander referred to his cages as a "Rat Park." Like the rats that overdosed alone in their cages, the rats in Rat Park were also offered water and heroin-laced water, but, unlike the lonely rats, the rats in Rat Park chose regular water. Though this example is overly simplistic and has been questioned (apparently, Alexander's experiment has not been replicated), it is still worth considering. Of course humans aren't rats and our lives are rarely in happy stress-free situations, but the overarching conclusion we might be able to take away from the Rat Park experiment is, that having a supportive environment will lead to better outcomes even if there may be genetic predispositions to the contrary (Alexander 2010). This conclusion seems to concur with the many memoirs of those with an SUD:

> I also longed to be close to my family again...he [a brother] launched a full-scale campaign to get me home. He whipped out his wallet: what will it take to get you back? Most of us need to push away from families at some point, and there's nothing wrong with that. But there's also nothing wrong with wanting them close again. Many people choose alternate families in sobriety. I chose my real one instead. (Hepola 2015, p.168)

It appears support and constancy, rather than punishment and rejection, yield better recovery outcomes for individuals with addiction (Livingston *et al.* 2012). The common wisdom among treatment providers now is to reduce rather than increase shame in order to yield improved results for those grappling with addiction. This is not a hard premise to support, as many parents of children with an ASD know. Rather than punishing a child with an ASD for tantrumming or acting out, parents often revamp their child's immediate environment in order to best accommodate the child's sensory as well as organizational needs, to reduce the child's stress, and allow them a chance to achieve therapeutic and educational goals (Mesibov and Shea 2010).

Recently other models regarding addictions have surfaced; one that is provocative in regards to this book is Maia Szalavitz's *Unbroken Brain: A Revolutionary New Way of Understanding Addiction* (2016). Szalavitz offers the premise that a substance use diagnosis is something akin to an autism diagnosis. Szalavitz even coopted the old ASD adage, "if you've met one person with autism, you've met one person with autism," and applied it to addictions. Szalavitz notes: "I find it really annoying when people say 'all addicts do X or Y.' Well, maybe you do X or Y, but don't speak for me" (quoted in Seigel 2016). Like having a diagnosis of autism, the individuals with a substance use diagnosis have a lot have a lot in common with one another and yet, remain enigmatic and unique. For example, those working in autism services would often remark on the commonality of an intense devotion by the preschool clients to *Thomas the Tank Engine*, but would also marvel over a particular child's intense interest in a specific unexpected subject such as house music or supernovas. In the field of substance abuse treatment there is a similar mix of commonalities and particularities. Anecdotally, some of the commonalities are the age and motivation that lure an individual to substances (it is not uncommon to find that those struggling with life-long addictions started their substance use between the ages of 12 and 14, and did so mostly to achieve social comfort and acceptance), but then there are the singular differences. For example, some patients who developed substance use problems did so due to specific traumas, and can pinpoint when they first picked up a drink or needle, while others eased into addiction without any conscious realization that they had developed a dependence until they were emotionally and physically entangled.

While investigating the roots of SUD, though many theories seem equally plausible, ultimately the most accurate explanation appears to be a targeted, individualized amalgam of various explanations that match the particular patient who is struggling with an addiction. Again, this amalgam of explanations is similar to those with an autism diagnosis. And like an ASD, there appears to be no specific cure but rather, forms of adaptation. Some former substance users claim they no longer use because they are strong-willed, and others attribute their abstinence to God. Many claim having social support is what made it possible for them to quit, while several others suggested that receiving an accurate mental health diagnosis along with appropriate treatment for that diagnosis essentially cured their cravings.

Another component of substance use is the building up of tolerance. People who don't drink or drink very little might find the rates of consumption for someone who has been abusing alcohol for years, say, a fifth of whiskey plus six to twelve beers a day, unthinkable. But for someone who has been abusing alcohol for ten or twenty years, that amount may seem perfectly normal.

Tolerance is a very real component of drug use, and often poor financial, health, and cognitive outcomes for substance abusers are the result of developing a higher tolerance. If that one glass of Merlot would offer those with substance dependence the same buzz they had when they started to drink, outcomes would most likely be significantly different. Tolerance and physical or mental withdrawal without the substance are signs that someone may have a substance use problem (APA 2013). These two indicators of SUD can be dangerous in that often individuals and professionals use these two telltale signs alone to assess if someone may have a problem. The risk is that there are other indicators that may be overlooked (Office of the Surgeon General 2016). There is the additional risk that treatment will not be ongoing once withdrawal is addressed. There appears to be a common misconception that once the physical symptoms of addiction are addressed, say, in a detox facility, the substance abuse issues are resolved. Detox is not the equivalent of treatment. Evidence suggests that additional treatment such as inpatient substance abuse treatment, intensive outpatient treatment, mental health counseling, and/or peer support such as AA/NA, Rational Recovery, or SMART are essential for maintaining recovery after physical withdrawal is complete and tolerance has lowered (SAMHSA 2016c). Detox is the first step prior to treatment; the goal is to help an individual withdraw safely from their substance of choice. Detox without follow-up treatment can not only lead to relapse, but it can also be lethal since overdoses often occur after leaving a detox facility without proper follow-up treatment when the addiction is still psychologically active but tolerance for drugs and alcohol has lowered (Strang *et al.* 2003).

The number of heroin users in the US has more than tripled in the past ten years (US Office on Drugs and Crime 2016). Does this have any impact on the ASD community? It might. Though many may not see the opioid epidemic as a threat to those with ASD, they might want to reconsider. Recently a mother of a young man with an ASD shared that after his wisdom teeth were extracted he was given a prescription for 20 Oxycontin. He dutifully followed his dentist's instructions and had the prescription filled and then proceeded to take the dosage on the bottle, even though the drugs made him feel "out of it." Since he was living with his parents at that time, his mother quickly stopped his intake, but if she hadn't, it is hard to know if he would have begun to enjoy how he felt on opioids. Would he have been more comfortable at work and around his peers? Would his usual anxiety have diminished? A heroin user recently confided that he started with Oxycodone, but once he was using it several times a day and his prescriptions were no longer refilled, he turned to heroin because it was easy for him to get and much cheaper. When asked why he continued to use heroin, he said: "It was the first time I felt normal. There's a reason they call it *a fix*. I just felt human for the first time" (Anonymous, personal communication, October 19, 2017). This falls in line with a posting on an online chat about an individual with an ASD's drug use:

> I have read similar posts but nothing dealing directly with autism and drug abuse (mainly opiates).
>
> My crazy guinea pig is autistic and currently in his third year as a history major at a university and not coincidently in his third year of narcotics use/addiction. That guinea pig loved pain killers, mainly Vicodin but he wouldn't pass up an Oxy or Codeine if it was around.
>
> My friendly guinea pig pretty much followed the textbook case—got a prescription for his terrible headaches, one fun day a week turned into a daily habit. He sold his stuff (he misses the xbox360) and ignored the bills. It was evident he had a problem that had to be fixed, etc… So now he is on Suboxone and has been clean for 30 days (unless you count Sub…).
>
> Apart from the detox, lack of sleep, Post Acute Withdrawal Symptoms, nostalgia for the pills, and on down the list, that weirdo guinea pig for the first time noticed the drilling thoughts and problematic emotions that are part of autism growing back inside of him. He has had 30 long days of soberness to think about this and realized what narcotics meant to him.
>
> Hydrocodone was the lost guinea pig's way of masking his autism and living a daily life. Taking a few pills allowed the poor guy to go to class and not be bothered by his headaches, the poor lighting, uncomfortable seats, movement of classmates, or the bothersome noises of dragging chalk and pencils. (Drugs-Forum 2009)

A parent of a child with an ASD once said that despite her son's father's struggles with alcohol, she was confident he would never become an alcoholic given his sensory issues and limited diet. In this day and age, when parents are mainstreaming their children and social expectations can be high, this mother's conclusions might be naive. Many young adults share that they dislike the taste of alcohol but don't mind the new sugary malt Alcopops that have inundated the alcohol market in the US. Many parents are not really aware of the prevalence of these inexpensive youth-oriented drinks, and often confuse them with the wine coolers of the 1980s and 1990s. But these sweet fizzy 16–25 ounce single-sized cans and bottles, with names like Mike's Hard Lemonade, Bud Light's Mang-o-Rita, Not Your Father's Root Beer or Twisted Tea Hard Ice Tea, are clearly being marketed to young people and contain much higher levels of alcohol than beer, wine, or wine coolers (Alcohol Justice and the San Rafael Alcohol & Drug Coalition 2015). It's easy for an individual who enjoys a glass of lemonade, fruit juice, or soda to consume alcohol without too much sensory discomfort, especially if it offers them the added bonus of an inexpensive means to facilitate social inclusion, temporarily alleviate social inhibition, justify social awkwardness, create a new persona, or allow for a cool detached demeanor when around an unreliable cohort.

> I was always picked on, couldn't retain friends or build up the courage to leave the comfort of home. I always felt that people were extremely mean to me, still do often, and fall victim to being taken advantage of. However, after a car accident I was prescribed pain meds. Mind you I've taken them responsibly for 4 years now, but I'm hooked and feel without them my newer "me" would die. Somehow I can now interact better and I'm more confident. I've made several friends, even found a beautiful wife. I am not condoning their use for that purpose but speculating that opiates may trigger something in our brains that we cannot naturally do on our own. I'd like to see more research done. I've looked many times and cannot find much on the subject. (Rosie's Quest 2013)

Adolescents and adults who develop substance use problems are more likely to have a co-occurring mental health diagnosis (SAMHSA 2016a). Much of the literature comparing dual diagnoses have argued that there is no link between ASD and SUD, with some articles even labeling autism as a protective factor for alcohol or drug addiction (Carey *et al.* 2016). One of the few ASD/SUD studies had different outcomes in that they found a low rate of illegal drug addiction and a higher rate of alcohol use. The study concluded that alcohol is legal and easily accessible, but individuals with an ASD may not be able to navigate the more complex social communicative skills needed to attain illegal substances (Kronenberg *et al.* 2014). This same article goes on to surmise that the problems adults with an ASD face every day might make alcohol a legal and easily accessible means of self-medication.

The Anxiety and Depression Association of America notes that about 20 percent of those with an anxiety or mood disorder (such as depression) have an SUD (2016). It is suspected that 40 percent of individuals with an ASD with an average or above-average IQ are diagnosed with anxiety, and 34 percent are diagnosed with clinical depression (Iadarola *et al.* 2016). With these statistics in mind, a case could be made that individuals with autism who have co-occurring depression or anxiety may be at risk for addictions. It could be argued that a percentage of adults, especially older adults, diagnosed with anxiety or depression may have undiagnosed autism and abused substances as a means to cope. In *Asperger Syndrome and Alcohol: Drinking to Cope?* (2008), Tinsley, whose autism was diagnosed after he had become dependent on alcohol, and Hendrickx, his therapist, declare: "The premise of this book is that those with AS [Asperger's Syndrome] are more prone to social anxiety disorders, and that research has shown that those with social anxiety are more than twice as likely to self-medicate with alcohol" (p.87). But it is important to also consider that even for those who know they have an autism diagnosis and have been mainstreamed, they might misuse alcohol or drugs to help them to integrate into a neurotypical world, especially if they are also grappling with depression and/or anxiety. As a YouTube poster shares:

> I have very poor social skills my entire life due to Asperger's syndrome and because I have poor social skills... I developed really bad social anxiety... I knew I had poor social skills and I came off as being aloof and as being unusual and what I learned years ago, that you know drinking a lot—alcohol—helped me better in social situations. It helped me with the social anxiety and helped make me be more comfortable with the fact I had poor social skills. It didn't actually help with the social skills, at all, but it made me feel like it did and it also made me more comfortable that I lacked social skills. (Soluna 2016)

A substance use diagnosis is not necessarily an equal opportunity condition since there can be genetic, social, clinical, and neurological components that make certain individuals more vulnerable to addiction than others, but it is a disservice to individuals with an ASD and/or their caregivers to assume the autism is a protective factor. There are very few studies exploring a connection (or lack thereof) between and ASD and SUD, and these studies can contradict one another, with some concluding rates of substance abuse are higher or lower for those with an ASD. In a 2016 study of tobacco and cannabis use in individuals diagnosed with pervasive developmental disorder (PDD), a diagnosis that is often synonymous with an ASD, the findings showed that the rates of tobacco and cannabis use among those with PDD were much lower than individuals with other psychiatric disorders, but then the researchers casually went on to share: "The rate of smoking in PDD patients is similar to that of the general population" (Schapir *et al.* 2016, p.1418). In this case, it is clear that PDD is not a protective factor. In his foreword to *Sex, Drugs and Asperger's Syndrome* (2014), Tony Attwood, when referring to those among his patients seeking drug and alcohol treatment, observes that both drugs and alcohol are more readily available than ever before. What we can also say is that more and more children diagnosed with an ASD are being mainstreamed and are, in a sense, also more readily available to social situations, peer pressures, relationship issues, school and employment successes and failures, etc. It is easy to underestimate the connection between substance use and autism because other populations, like those diagnosed with ADHD, eclipse society's attention with much higher rates of SUD than the general population. We need to keep in mind that somewhere around 50 percent of those with an ASD manifest symptoms of ADHD, and over two-thirds of individuals with ADHD have features of autism (Leitner 2014).

Developmental delays can be seen as a protective factor for substance abuse, and in certain circumstances they are, but there is also the propensity to infantilize those with disabilities, assuming that the problems those without documented disabilities face may not impact what was once a sheltered population. Teens and young adults with an ASD may seem well protected because their parents and loved ones might be more attentive, but family involvement does not guarantee safety. Family members and professionals should be mindful of all the possible dangers that befall neurotypical teens and adults, not just the concerns most commonly associated with those with an ASD such as bullying, struggles in school, or vocational challenges. Individuals with an ASD may have the added protection of being monitored more than most teens and young adults, but substance use should not be ignored. The dangers of addiction need to be added to the list of other regularly addressed concerns such as bullying, academic challenges, or employment. What many self-advocates already know is that along with the many positive outcomes for those with an ASD due to the advent of disability rights and legislation, such as the Individuals with Disabilities Education Act (IDEA), mainstreaming and inclusion can expose those with disabilities to the benefits and

detriments associated with typical human development. It is important
to remind ourselves that the biological, environmental, and social risks
for developing substance use problems can impact all populations.

CHAPTER 2

USING SUBSTANCES TO COPE

After a hard day, it's common to have a drink to unwind. Most people who drink or do drugs do so casually: to relax, chill out, de-stress, transition, decompress, escape. That is, drinking or using to cope—to cope with daily stressors, the shift from work to home, with a houseful of children. A glass of red wine is recommended for health; a toke can relieve anxiety. Of course, alcohol and drugs aren't always used as a means to manage stress. Sometimes substances are used to have fun, to enhance already pleasurable moments, to add a ritualistic quality to an event, or to celebrate. But most often alcohol and drugs are used to cope, that is, to deal with a difficult situation effectively. Substance use disorder is often seen as a coping mechanism run amok. Nobody plans to become addicted. We might start using substances to cope and eventually cannot cope without the substance. As noted earlier in this book, individuals with an autism spectrum diagnosis have higher rates of anxiety and depression. It is hard to tease out whether the stress of managing socially and emotionally in a neurotypical world causes anxiety and depression or exacerbates pre-existing, underlying anxiety and depression, but either way, people with autism, like anyone else dealing with stress, may well desire to drink or use drugs to cope. Tessie Regan, in *Shorts: Stories about Alcohol, Asperger Syndrome, and God*, remembers:

> ...I was 13 and I found alcohol. The bitter magic seemed to grease the squeaky and rusty cogs and wheels in my head. Things ran smoothly. Things got quiet. Things in the world seemed more approachable and real. Less like the fragile, sensory-imploding world that went unchallenged when dry and sober. (2014, p.13)

PROTECTIVE FACTORS OF AUTISM

When considering the protective and risk factors of autism in relation to substance abuse and dependence, the protective factors appear to outweigh the risk factors. For example, many with an ASD tend to be strict rule-followers, and the idea of crossing the line or breaking the law would be untenable. Even the basic primary and secondary school teachings that drugs are a bad choice may be repeated by some with an ASD:

> When I was in high school (in the early 70s), the school brought in (allegedly) former druggies to speak to us about the hazards of drug use. Someone asked about the residual effects, and we were told that short-term memory is still a problem long after marijuana use stops. I have always had such a problem with my short-term memory that I wouldn't have dared to mess with it. (Blogger.com 2009)

Sensory sensitivities could make the taste of alcohol too unpleasant to pursue. Snorting, smoking, or intravenous drug use, a turn-off to those with mild neurotypical sensory issues, might be abhorrent to individuals with autism. Experimentation, seen as deviation from a regular routine, might not be welcomed, and if one does experiment, not feeling oneself in a world where there is a need to blend in could be especially unnerving:

> ...as per previous post "I wish I didn't have Asperger's syndrome," if I could pick whether I had the condition or not, it's hard to say either way, I don't wish I didn't have the condition, I just wish I didn't have some of the negative aspects of of [sic] the condition. And alcohol if [sic] one of the ways I can get rid of these negative aspects. The venues of substance use may also be too hard to adjust to; noisy crowded bars or late night fraternity parties may be close to impossible for an individual who has sensory modulation issues. People with ASD who have limited social networks would not have the wherewithal to know where to seek out and access illegal substances. (Smith 2012)

And the financial constraints that impact many with an ASD, such as low rates of employment, would also have an impact on an individual's ability to maintain the high cost of substance use, especially as one becomes more tolerant and needs a higher quantity of a substance to get high. "I was drinking 8 pints a night 7 days a week, but cut down to 4 days a week in January because I couldn't afford…" (Keay 2017).

MAINSTREAMING: THE BENEFITS AND RISKS

When a child is diagnosed with autism, some of these protective factors such as heightened sensory responses, lack of social engagement, or rigid routinized behaviors are seen as deficits and are routinely treated as such. Given the recent efforts of families, schools, and therapists to ameliorate some of these characteristics, and the progress that has been made, it is no longer possible to assume these protective factors will still be in play when the child grows into an adult. In fact, those protective factors may well become risk factors, as mainstreaming is now the current goal. In the past, those diagnosed with autism and other developmental delays might have been shuttled off to institutions or special schools. Work, higher education, or a home in the community may not have been an expectation or even an option. Today, via the passage of the much-needed Individuals with Disabilities Education Act (IDEA) in 1975, and its updated reauthorization in 2004, and the passage of the American with Disabilities Act (ADA) in 1990, the landscape for individuals with developmental disabilities has altered considerably. Though the differently-abled still have a long way to go in terms of equal access, these two federal laws have significantly improved the landscape for those diagnosed with a developmental disability. But as we all know, progress can bring unexpected challenges. Colleges are now expected to enroll and accommodate the needs of young adults who may be intellectually capable of reaping the benefits of a college education, but may not have the social maturity to connect to their typically developing cohort:

> Part of what made college so exhausting was my proneness to get lost in the details. One detail of a lesson, lecture, assignment, or test question would grab my focus and I would lose sight of the whole picture. If one word was wrong in a sentence or oddly placed, I was so consumed by that one small detail that I completely lost sight of what the text said making me have to go back and re-read the entire thing. I could not stay focused.
>
> I suspect that my autism bubbled up to the surface highlighting many of the core deficits that those with Asperger's Syndrome (AS), Autism Spectrum Disorders (ASD), and High-Functioning

Autism (HFA) share. I clearly had severe deficits with Theory of Mind, but college life made my weak central coherence and executive dysfunction noticeable. (Davide-Rivera 2012)

With the advent of federal student aid and various incentive grants for specialized programs tailored to those with autism via the Higher Education Opportunity Act of 2008, there is now an abundance of special high school and higher education programs for individuals with an ASD. Disability services offices are becoming more prominent mainstays of the college landscape. The mandate for many of these facilities is to assist individuals with an ASD among others to achieve academic success. In the US, vocational rehabilitation (VR) supports individuals with an ASD and other disabilities by offering skills training for appropriate employment and assistance procuring jobs. VR, and other services like it (job coaching, tutoring, career counseling, or educational or academic coaching) may touch on the social and emotional strains that may go along with success in school or at work, but the ultimate goal is academic or vocational achievement rather than enhanced social interactions and emotional wellbeing.

Yeah, we Aspies can be employed. But we switch jobs constantly, and the jobs we work almost inevitably play to our weaknesses—i.e. menial, uninteresting, repetitive tasks and social interaction (retail). We get used to being fired for nebulous "performance" reasons (i.e. oddness, social difficulty). So, it's as much about the fact of employment as it is about the quality of employment, and that person's resulting quality of life. I was fired 2 years ago from a job due directly to an Aspie symptom—all of which are more pervasive when under stress—illiteracy of a social situation, and being tricked & taken advantage of by a dishonest customer. (Bollard 2011)

SOCIAL ANXIETY

Anyone with social anxiety or social awkwardness knows that alcohol can be, as a person with autism noted, "a great leveler." This same person went on to praise alcohol because "It removes their [a group's] ability to recognize social cues, thus rendering us even. I could never deal with people when I was sober" (SoberRecovery Forums July 31, 2012). In *Asperger Syndrome and Alcohol: Drinking to Cope?*, Tinsley and Hendrickx (2008, p.22) describe alcohol as a "numbing device which enables tolerance, integration, acceptance and flexibility, which the person with AS [Asperger's Syndrome] may not naturally possess."

Other medications that might offer similar though slightly less expeditious results would be opioids such as Vicodin, Percocet, or Heroin, or benzodiazepines (benzos) such as Klonopin, Valium, or Ativan. These prescribed pain relievers or antianxiety medications are controlled but frequently abused substances that are highly addictive and, one hopes, meted out warily by physicians. Tinsley did not know he had autism until he had become addicted to alcohol. He explains in his book that he drank to self-medicate. This points out a distinction (that appears to be generational) among many adults with autism—there are two specific groups of adolescents/adults with an ASD at risk for SUD—those who know they have a diagnosis but who have been raised to be mainstreamed and to seamlessly blend into the general population, and those who reached adulthood having never received an autism diagnosis. Later in this book we address the differences and similarities between these two groups, and whether one might be more or less prone to become addicted to drugs or alcohol, but what this information does tell us is that, by the time they reach adulthood, both groups are expected to cope with the various social and emotional stressors prevalent in the neurotypical landscape.

> Back in 2002, I was married, in full-time employment and most significantly, a heavy drinker. I had never heard of Asperger's Syndrome. The following year my marriage broke up and I lost my job, due mostly to my drinking. I used alcohol to deal with the overwhelming sense of anxiety which I had had since childhood. I had also abused tranquilizers to help cope with the levels of fear and stress I experienced in day-to-day life. (Tinsley 2017)

Temple Grandin, in her introduction to Tinsley and Hendrickx's (2008) book, shares: "At important work social events I always used to have a few drinks because it calmed me down" (pp.7–8). Of course, Grandin is no different from most typical adults at a social function who might be uncomfortable, and, like the majority of the population, she knows that the urge to drink to function comfortably socially needs to be kept in check, otherwise she might become addicted. So people with autism, like people without autism, find alcohol and other drugs helpful for fitting in, for the social anxiety associated with assimilating and managing the stress and depression that comes along with navigating adulthood and independence.

As mentioned earlier, these same stressors are abundant for neurotypical adolescents and adults. We are not saying that these stressors are any different, but we are willing to assert that they might be more prevalent and intense for someone with autism.

> Life with Asperger's is like living with Dolby Surround sound, wearing 3-D glasses like those used in movie theaters, and having your sense of smell and touch jacked up to the max. Simple things like going to the grocery store or a restaurant are anxiety-proving events that only we can understand. (Attwood *et al.* 2014, p.111)

SOCIAL CAPITAL VIA DRUGS AND ALCOHOL

In certain circles, there is also social capital to be gained by using drugs and drinking alcohol. In the 1980s, when the economy was booming, cocaine was considered glamorous, particularly in upper middle-class white society. This was the climate when Maia Szalavitz (2016, pp.123–124), then a freshman at Columbia University, embarked on her addictions:

> I was exposed to the upper class for the first time. I had no idea how to fit in... I had a constant sense that I was walking around without knowing that I had toilet paper on my shoe or chocolate at the corners of my mouth; something about me was always not quite right...back then I had no clue how to be or at least feel more acceptable. What I did know, however, was that drugs were a valuable social currency. And that was how, in short order, I began to sell coke. The drug had become extremely glamorously popular...as long as I had coke, I knew that I was wanted. It's hard to feel left out when everyone is waiting for you to arrive.

In their study regarding substance use and Asperger's Syndrome, Clarke, Tickle, and Gillott (2016) hit on a significant discrepancy in past studies regarding substance use among individuals on the autism spectrum. Most studies did not factor in a desire for social interaction when studying motivation for substance use: "...previous literature that has inferred that the social difficulties experienced by individuals on the autistic spectrum is a protective factor against SUD development is erroneous, and in fact, may be a risk factor for socially orientated individuals" (Clarke *et al.* 2016, p.160). "I am in college and have no real friends there, I crave alcohol because I think if I could just drink I could go to bars and meet people my own age" (SoberRecovery Forums February 4, 2008).

Very few studies or writings regarding the relationship between an ASD and SUD account for the social capital achieved by using, and, in Szalavitz's case, dealing drugs. As Clarke *et al.* (2016) acknowledge, there is a sub-group of adults with an ASD who have an intense desire to socialize and fit in. These individuals may have the added burden of knowingly breaking the law in order to maintain the social capital they have gained via their use of illegal substances. The cognitive dissonance of betraying a society's rules in order to feel included in that neurotypical society may increase feelings of indignity for the person using. Adding rule-breaking to the mix may make for additional shame that can feed addictions:

> What worries me, if we can go back to the autistic mindset for a second, is that autistic people are often social justice-oriented and strict rule-followers. So if they internalize these policies—even though they don't make rational sense—then it's really not going to help their self-esteem if they get into a situation where they're addicted to illegal drugs. (Des Roches Rosa 2016)

THE CONSEQUENCES OF MISSED SOCIAL CUES

It is critical to tease out these commonalities and differences of those who have an autism diagnosis. And it is equally important to acknowledge the layers and nuances too, when we make these assertions. There are those with an ASD who may not have a desire to socialize, may be indifferent to or unaware of what other people think, may not have any interest whatsoever in fitting in. Indeed, this particular portrait of autism appears to be the most common among the public and professionals. In fact, recent trends in research have emphasized that social motivation or social rewards have a minimal impact on the behavior of individuals with an ASD (Chevallier *et al.* 2012; Damiano *et al.* 2012). Given this current view, autism is seen as a protective factor regarding SUD (Clarke *et al.* 2016). But we should not discount the risks for unexpected social stressors for individuals with this particular profile. An adult with autism who is doing well statistically—that is, employed and living independently—and who has no desire to fit in socially may find that sitting on a bench on the way home from work is an effective way to transition from job-life to home-life. What if the bench is near a small playground and a concerned parent finds the sight of a full-grown man alone at the playground odd and unnerving and calls the police?[1] What if the police question this young man and, when asked why he was on the bench, he has no other answer than, "I like it." What if the officer tells this young man that he can no longer sit alone on the bench? What if this young man needs another avenue of release, or what if this young man, who still may not understand how he is perceived and the implications of his utterly innocent actions, interprets the officer's instructions literally to mean avoid the bench he was on, and so, chooses to go to another bench on the other side of that playground, or to a bench at another park with children, and is subsequently arrested for the town's ordinance against adults alone in public children's play areas? To a person with an ASD or the loved one of a person with an ASD, this scenario may resonate. Other scenarios are also possible: what if the police officer handles the adult with an ASD roughly? What if the person who initially reported the man at the playground confronts him harshly without accounting for his lack of understanding? People with autism can be incarcerated for their odd or seemingly indifferent behaviors:

> ...When I spoke to the police in my usual rather direct way, they thought I was being rude. I told the police I had Asperger syndrome and asked if I could get a friend who could help me to explain myself, but they did not seem to understand the condition and I was told that I couldn't. At this stage I became very nervous and tried to get away. In response, they called for back-up and tried to arrest me. When they tried to put the handcuffs on me it felt like an invasion of my space. I felt anxious and so the situation worsened. They shoved me into a van. I felt so scared that I responded by biting an officer. (National Autism Society 2014, p.13)

Although this example may seem extreme, Robertson and MacGillivray (2015) suspect there is an overrepresentation of individuals with an ASD in prison settings. Similar conclusions are beginning to arise

---

1   Some town ordinances are as follows: "Adults are allowed in designated children play areas in the city only when accompanied by a minor. Children play areas where this section is applicable will be specifically designated and signs will be posted informing the public of the designation" (Kozlowski 2015).

regarding the prevalence rates of individuals with an ASD and SUD (indeed, many individuals with an ASD in the criminal justice system have drug/alcohol-related charges against them; see Cashin and Newman 2009). Aspects associated with an ASD that could be seen as protective factors for an SUD, such as discomfort in social situations or rule-following, may also be risk factors. Adolescents and adults with an ASD who may seem indifferent to the social expectations that neurotypical adults encounter find themselves in unexpectedly stressful situations needing to find a means to cope.

> I didn't start developing any real social skills until I was about 21. When I'm with people, I can usually put on a good show of being friendly and relaxed, however this "fake" personality can be very exhausting at times, and has never allowed me to truly connect with anyone, so as a result I don't have any friends at all, and very few people around me that I can talk to. My only friends are my dogs and alcohol. (SoberRecovery Forums July 5, 2008)

Being literal and following rules may have the potential for a person with an ASD to lead to misunderstandings, adding unexpected anxiety. Given the accessibility of alcohol and the growing accessibility of marijuana, it does not seem farfetched to speculate that these substances could be a means to reduce everyday stress as well as the unexpected stresses that may arise:

> I've used marijuana to help me with the social issues. I can go from nearly incapable of going to anything that has the slightest issue in my head to outright enthusiasm on it (nearly)... Sadly I learnt that there is a risk of becoming quite attached (not addicted). You do get a desire to feel so comfortable every day, especially when your aspergers is a near constant obstacle.
>
> I've decided to take a month's break. After which I plan to use it purely to help me when I need to do social occasions... Though I don't see it helping in the long term, as coming down from marijuana after much use can actually increase depression. But I can't tell whether that's just a result of experiencing life with less aspergers, then going back to having more. So be always prepared that you will return to the struggle. I also use buddhist meditation to maintain a simplistic and rational mind-space, and marijuana can kind of damage that rational mind-space if it's abused. (Blogger.com 2009)

UNDERSTANDING SELF-MEDICATION

Of course, like neurotypical adults, people with an ASD may try drugs or alcohol and find it's just not for them. What we are arguing is, like neurotypical adults, people with an ASD may find alcohol and drugs are exactly the right thing, and people with an ASD are not immune to the lure of self-medication. Tim Page (2009), in his memoir about growing up with undiagnosed Asperger's, describes his later teen years: "I always needed to escape myself, and this was the only period in my life where I was a dawn-to-dusk drinker, for the panic attacks would set in the moment the booze wore off" (Page 2009, p.156).

It is important to understand what self-medication might actually mean in this context. It could be understood in many different ways depending on the individual and their circumstances. Self-medication usually carries with it overtones of negativity, referring to an individual's misuse of drugs, alcohol, or other substances (and in broader terms, actions such as video-gaming or overeating) to alleviate symptoms of mental or physical illnesses. What is important to recognize is that we all self-medicate to one degree or another—we take a cold pill for a stuffy nose, an antacid for a sour stomach, an aspirin for a headache, a cup of coffee as a pick-me-up, or vitamins to supplement our diet. Self-medicating for emotional problems is frowned upon because the choices of medications tend to be sketchier. But with the pharmaceutical companies aiming for huge profits, wining and dining medical professionals, and advertising their wares on television as if the drugs they are selling are no different than a magic mop or a bag of frozen vegetables, it is acceptable to be skeptical of the professional alternatives offered. Self-medication truly means to choose medicines oneself without "expert advice." Context is important; for example, the World Health Organization (WHO 2000) report on self-medication addresses some of the potential benefits as: "…Wider availability of medicines; Greater choice of treatment; Direct, rapid access to treatment; An active role in his or her own health care; Self-reliance in preventing or relieving minor symptoms or conditions…" (p.11). But it doesn't shy away from the potential pitfalls, including: "…Failure to recognize or report adverse drug reactions; Incorrect route or manner of administration; Inadequate or excessive dosage; Excessively prolonged use; Risk of dependence and abuse…" (WHO 2000, p.12).

Sometimes, we bandy about the term "self-medication" or "self-help" when referring to activities such as exercise or meditation. Exercise, meditation, prayer, peer groups, and other activities that help with focus, stress, mental, and physical health might be considered part of a person's overall treatment used alone or in tandem with medications. Interestingly, these non-pharmacological alternatives can be an effective alternative for medication. In fact, studies have shown that particular forms of therapy and meditation, such as mindfulness—a clinical secular form of meditation—in conjunction with cognitive behavioral therapy (CBT), prove to be as effective in treating major depressive disorder in the general adult population as antidepressant medications (Creswell 2016). And when addressing SUD, mindfulness has been shown to be beneficial for treating cravings related to substance abuse and relapse (Kozasa *et al.* 2016). Therefore, it could be said that self-medication can be used to treat self-medication, or, to put it another way, some forms of self-medication are healthy while others, usually done in excess, are not. It is clear self-medication is a nuanced and complicated concept, particularly in connection with an ASD and SUD, and we address this again and in more detail later in this book.

It is important to tease out if self-medication is, as Tinsley and Hendrickx assert (2008), an escape from pain, or whether it does offer genuine relief. Could self-medication mean using illicit substances and/or alcohol to open or close receptors in the brain affected by one's disorder? That is to say, could self-medication be an effective treatment for symptoms of an individual's health disorder?

> Cannabis is an excellent medicine for combating the symptoms of Asperger's, I've been using it medically myself since I was 24, and I'm 28 now. It's the only medicine that works for me; as small a dose as I want, no headaches or sickness, no awful side effects. (Aspies Central 2017)

For example, individuals with a diagnosis of schizophrenia are significantly more prone to use marijuana than the general population (Compton, Furman, and Kaslow 2004). It appears that the choice to smoke or ingest cannabis is more complicated than simply an attempt to treat the symptoms of their disease. First, there is a debate among professionals as to whether the use of marijuana might trigger schizophrenia in individuals (Radhakrishnan, Wilkinson, and D'Souza 2015), or if individuals prone to schizophrenia are seeking out marijuana to treat their illness (Cassidy *et al.* 2014). Recent research regarding these connections has received attention due to current laws legalizing marijuana use. If the claims that marijuana use can trigger schizophrenia in adolescents genetically prone to the disorder are true, and given the mode marijuana is being sold in some states (cookies, brownies, and other sweets), these particular concerns have greater weight with the prospect of cannabis becoming easily accessible to minors. Meanwhile, researchers are still teasing apart the chicken and egg questions of whether marijuana use causes psychosis, or if psychosis makes people want to get high (Volkow *et al.* 2014). To add to this complicated scenario, studies have emerged mapping brain responses in both schizophrenia and marijuana use. Some studies have found that the THC (Tetrahydrocannabinolin, principal psychoactive constituent) in marijuana is detrimental to those prone to schizophrenia and can aggravate symptoms, while the Cannabidiol in marijuana can be beneficial and alleviate symptoms (Leweke *et al.* 2012). This is all to say that the term *self-medication* may have many different meanings, and it is important to take this into account when exploring drug/alcohol use, especially among those who have differently wired brains, such as individuals with an ASD. As Tim Page (2009, p.110) attests: "I had by then been diagnosed with Asperger's syndrome and, once I returned to wine again, it felt as though I had reintroduced a central solvent that my body chemistry had been missing..." For Page, alcohol is the cure for his anxiety. We therefore need to be open to the possibility that self-medication for some may actually be medication.

COPING VERSUS DEPENDENCY OR ADDICTION

Coping is how we respond to stress so that we maintain mental health and, subsequently, emotional wellbeing. *Drinking to Cope?*, the subtitle of Tinsley and Hendrickx's (2008) book about Asperger's and alcohol, postulates that having undiagnosed autism was the root of the co-author's alcohol dependence. And in Tinsley's case, this may well be true, but for those in the SUD field, dependence on substances is much more complicated and subtle. Yes, we may well pick up a drink or turn to a pill during times of emotional stress, we may even find the result of consuming that drink or pill to be exactly as we hoped—a means to cope—but addiction is a much more tangled and tricky outcome than merely the byproduct of continuous self-soothing. There are a number of factors that lead to addiction, including one's familial background, brain chemistry, trauma history, and support system. As mentioned earlier, SUD is the result of a complex assortment of personal risk factors that don't easily align when there is the need to cope. As Temple Grandin notes: "I could have easily fallen into the trap of becoming dependent on alcohol… To avoid having a problem, I never consumed alcohol in my house, but not everyone has the willpower to do this" (quoted in Tinsley and Hendrickx 2008, p.8). Willpower, a term often used for those who manage not to succumb to SUD, is another concept that is more complex than simply the strength to resist. Willpower is a combination of self-discipline and determination that is critical for resisting temptation, but knowing how willpower is structured in the brain is essential to understanding both addiction and autism. It could be said that the opposite of willpower is impulsivity, which treads into ADHD territory and, once again, it is clear that sometimes our brains are hijacked by their wiring. As Bechara (2005), in an article examining willpower, impulsivity, and drug use notes, not all of us are wired with willpower: "this mechanism enables one to endure sacrifices now in order to obtain benefits later, or vice versa" (p.1458). Sometimes it is difficult for any of us, especially if we're overwhelmed by extreme stress, to register the farsighted outcomes that willpower offers.

Adolescents and adults with autism do seem to be wired with a certain form of willpower, and we explore the pros and cons of that particular facet of ASD in more detail in the next chapter. This type of willpower—an uncanny ability to focus on a particular interest without succumbing to distraction, sometimes to the point of obsession—can be seen as a deterrent to SUD, while at the same time, the intensity of focus can read like an addiction. In other words, this single-mindedness can be both a liability and an asset depending on what the interest may be. Certainly, those with addictive behaviors have a single-mindedness that can be channeled into something productive, and this is often the strategy used for those with an ASD. In the case of substance abuse and ASD, we must remind ourselves to challenge our own assumptions of what an individual with autism might turn to for solace.

INTERNET USE OR GAMING

Currently the most commonly reported and addressed addiction among those with an ASD is digital media, particularly compulsive gaming. As MacMullin, Lunsky, and Weiss (2016, p.53) note, "…individuals with an ASD may be at a particularly high risk for problems related to electronics use, including excessive and problematic video game and Internet use." Though this book will not be addressing gaming and internet addictions, we can draw parallels between an SUD and compulsive gaming. In *The Loving Push* (2015), a guide to parenting children with autism to be successful adults, Grandin and Moore dedicate a chapter to the dangers of unchecked access to digital media consumption and compulsive gaming. They noted that children with an ASD enjoy online gaming because it satisfies unmet social needs packaged in a manner that autistic brains might prefer: "Instead of being bullied, ignored, or outcast, now your child has the opportunity to be a highly respected, valued person, even if it is in the form of their avatar" (Grandin and Moore 2015, p.116).

Given the plethora of literature surrounding gaming/technology misuse among individuals with autism, it appears to be the "drug" of choice for those with an ASD. Though this may be true, it may also be the most accessible means to cope or self-medicate, particularly for children. Many articles addressing overuse of the internet and gaming by adolescents and adults with an ASD suggest that those abusing technology should be redirected to advance their skills and interests via the internet—essentially turning the potential liabilities of this addiction into possible assets. Many articles conclude with a call for a "healthy" use of the internet:

> Virtual environments can assist individuals with social communication challenges in circumventing social barriers and developing meaningful relationships. In this environment the perceived constraints of social/communicative disorders like ASD do not inhibit effective communication or relevant social interactions. The universal proliferation of technology and the exponential growth in massively multiplayer online role-playing games provides an individual with social communication challenges the opportunity for typical social and participatory interactions for individuals participating in that type of gaming environment. (Gallup *et al.* 2016, p.235)

Those in the addictions field know that caution is necessary when redirecting addictive behaviors. A compulsive gambler may exclaim that they are cured and paying off their debts by working day and night—or becoming a "workaholic." There are those with autism who are fortunate enough to reroute their obsessions into something productive, but this is not a given. It is not easy to get that same dopamine rush that gaming or the internet offers those prone to compulsive gaming. As Grandin and Moore warn, "Biologically, gaming works like any other addicting drug" (2015, p.116).

CLINICAL AND FAMILIAL FOLLOW-UP

Alcohol and drugs can offer precisely what gaming offers—rituals and rules, escape, self-medication, a chance to socialize as a better version of oneself—essentially, a tempting, readily available means to cope. And as a social vehicle as well as a social lubricant, alcohol and some drugs can be the perfect medium for those with social anxiety and/or who lack the social skills to function in a neurotypical world. As one participant in Clarke *et al.*'s (2016, p.159) study put it: "It just takes the edge off the nasty feeling you get when you're trying to talk to somebody, that you feel stupid. You don't get that if you've had alcohol." Current research regarding the social aspects of autism propagates the profile of an individual with autism as one who is not inclined to reap the rewards of social interactions. This research implies that the desire for social interaction is less prevalent among those with an ASD as in the general population:

> The social world summons our attention like no other domain: social signals are prioritized by attention, interactions are intrinsically rewarding, and social maintaining permeates interpersonal behaviors... In ASD, by contrast, there appears to be an overall decrease in the attentional weight assigned to social information. Diminished social orienting, social reward and social maintaining, are all found in autism... (Chevallier *et al.* 2012, p.9)

Though this current research appears to prove, through brain imaging, that individuals with an ASD do not have the same circuitry that may respond to social rewards as those without an ASD, studies of adults and adolescents who misuse drugs and alcohol have found that the primary motivation for doing so was to fit in socially (Clarke *et al.* 2016). Our worry is that clinicians who work with individuals with an autism diagnosis might discount their desire for comfortable social interactions as motivation for their actions. The assumption that an adult with an ASD does not have the desire to socialize, to fit in, to feel accepted, may prevent a clinician from suspecting substance use or misuse among their clientele with an autism diagnosis. The same may be true for family members of the patient. Though screening for an SUD is common for many other mental health conditions, it is not routine for those with an ASD (Arnevik and Helverschou 2016). Mental health and addiction specialists need to ensure that their patients have accurate diagnoses and are receiving effective treatment. Self-advocates, family members, and clinicians need to keep in mind that, as one study found, individuals with an ASD were not getting proper treatment because professionals had a hard time teasing apart the complex manner in which an ASD and SUD can present (Arnevik and Helverschou 2016). Those working in substance abuse treatment should educate themselves to possible autistic traits or characteristics in order to assess if their clients might have an undiagnosed developmental or learning disability, and follow through by offering their clients comprehensive assessments in order to tailor their interventions appropriately. Ultimately it is critical that family members, friends, and professionals who have been focused on offering adolescents or adults with an ASD the skills to assimilate to a neurotypical world be aware of the potential for alcohol or drug misuse, and consider not only education regarding substance abuse, but also explore the possibility that substance abuse may already be in play.

CHAPTER 3

BEHAVIORAL CONNECTIONS BETWEEN AUTISM SPECTRUM DIAGNOSIS AND ADDICTION

Most parents of an autistic child learn the word "perseverate" fairly early on in the process of receiving an autism diagnosis or while seeking services for their child. To perseverate is to continue or to prolong a thought, action, or utterance long after the actual event that initiated it has ceased. We all perseverate, perhaps lying in bed and reflecting late into the evening, replaying and reimagining an event that may have happened earlier that day, having part of a song stuck in our head long after we've heard it, or longing for another high soon after the desired effect of the last high has worn off.

PERSEVERATIVE BEHAVIORS AND AUTISM

One hallmark of an ASD is perseveration. On the Geeky Science Mom's Tumblr blog (2013), the author explains her take on perseveration:

> Let's say you are autistic and you have a special interest in Ford Mustangs. A non-autistic person may read about them occasionally and know some important facts about the company and statistics of the car itself... A person on the autism spectrum will not only read about the Ford Mustang, but memorize all the

facts and statistics of the car and company and be able to tell others everything they know over and over again. Special interests can consume someone on the autism spectrum. Their special interest is all they can think about and all they can talk about. Every spare moment could potentially be used to focus on the special interest. It consumes them so much that it can potentially interfere with their lives. I know this, because I have lived with Aspergers all my life.

Another take on perseveration was offered in Cynthia Kim's Musings of an Aspie blog:

[Perseveration] is more of a "broken record" kind of repetition. It's asking someone the same question or making the same statement over and over, even though the other person has already answered or acknowledged it. I do this a lot...especially in relation to making plans. "Let's run tomorrow morning."

Ten minutes later: "Tomorrow is a running day, right?" A half hour later: "I want to run in the morning. Oh, wait, I said that already, didn't I?" Which doesn't stop me from wanting to say it another ten times as the evening wears on. (May 22, 2014)

Perseveration is one of many "atypical" behaviors connected to autism; it falls into the category of repetitive behaviors that also includes stereotypical noises and/or movements, also known as *stimming*, and habits and routines. Repetitive behavior is one of the three core symptoms of autism, along with language impairment and social deficits (Autism Speaks 2017d). These three categories are often accompanied by other neurological issues, such as mood and anxiety disorders as well as ADHD, problems with sleep, and OCD. It is important to note that the repetitive behaviors associated with autism and OCD may stem from anxiety, but the net results differ significantly. Perseveration and repetition in autism is, for the most part, a form of self-soothing that can mitigate anxiety, whereas the repetitive behaviors associated with OCD are primarily unwanted and distressing (APA 2013).

PERSEVERATIVE BEHAVIORS AND SUBSTANCE USE

In the previous chapter we explored self-medicating one's anxiety, depression, or social deficits as a possible cause of a substance use diagnosis for those with or without an ASD. But what if autism and a substance use diagnosis are biologically as well as psychologically linked? When we think of substance abuse and dependence there is often a core perseverative/repetitive component. In the substance abuse field there is talk of cravings or "desire thinking" (Caselli and Spada 2016). For many individuals with an SUD, cravings and triggers can be the source of continual relapse. It is common for those in recovery from an SUD to relapse due to seemingly unexplained triggers. Any unconscious stimuli might relate to when they were using: "…I would always end up leaving the table in the middle of a good meal or conversation just to indulge in more heroin use. So when I first entered into recovery, public bathrooms were a real trigger for me" (William 2016). In his textbook on drug use and treatment, Goldberg (2013) notes that the sight of white sugar or talcum powder could activate a craving in former cocaine addicts, even after years of successful abstinence. Are cravings related to repetitive behaviors in autism? In a study of Australian twins focused on the autistic traits of individuals (rather than an official autism diagnosis), the researchers found that those with behaviors associated with autism, such as communication challenges, social difficulties, and a desire to engage in repetitive behaviors, were more likely to abuse marijuana and alcohol (de Alwis *et al.* 2014). Indeed, the social deficits discussed in the previous chapter certainly put an individual at risk of addiction in order to cope with those deficits, but the de Alwis *et al.* article and others like it point to other underlying causes such as neurobiological similarities like repetitive behaviors that are inherent in both an ASD and SUD (Ghaziuddin 2005).

COMMONALITIES OF REPETITION IN AN ASD AND SUD

It is apparent that an SUD and an ASD have common features that may be biological in nature (van Wijngaarden-Cremers, Brink, and Gaag 2014, p.3): "They also share similarities at a behavioral level such as the level of detailed perception and rigid and compulsive habits." For example, both individuals with an SUD and ASD might have a very particular substance/interest that might lead them to take risks in order to pursue that substance/interest. This is clear with someone with an addiction to illegal substances who will risk the loss of employment, alienation from their loved ones, incarceration, and even death in order to pursue their addiction. An example of this single-minded pursuit for someone with autism might be something like the New York City resident with an ASD who has made headlines more than once for hijacking trains and buses due to his deep-seated interest in public transportation, and has even been quoted as saying, "I know there is no such program as Trains Anonymous, but if I can get some kind of counseling it would be really beneficial towards me" (Tietz 2002). This extreme example points out that those who want to pursue their "specialist subject" might do so without regarding the risk of possible addiction associated with pursuing their goal.

Even though the headlines and anecdotes of perseverative behaviors of those with an ASD are particular and quirky, the biological component that drives these behaviors appears to be inherently linked to the behaviors of those who abuse substances. Anyone who has had an addiction or has been around someone with an addiction knows that person is an "expert" in their drug of choice. Just like Geeky Science Mom Tumblr's (2013) description of someone with autism knowing all there is to know about Mustangs, someone who has depended on substances knows everything about their substance of choice, and it "is all they can think about and all they can talk about. Every spare moment could potentially be used to focus on the special interest. It consumes them…" Or, as an adult with an addiction to heroin shared, "It's [heroin] the first thing I think about when I wake up. Before I even open my eyes" (Anonymous, personal communication April 18, 2017).

REPETITIVE BEHAVIOR AND AUTISM

What are the different ways that repetitive behaviors manifest themselves in autism, and why do people with autism have repetitive behaviors? As noted earlier in this chapter, some people with an ASD might have a particular interest or, as Luke Jackson (2016) calls it, a *specialist subject*, and perseverate on it. But there are other ways that people with autism might display repetitive behaviors such as particular recurring physical movements or repeating a sound or phrase over and over. These stereotypical behaviors are known in the autism world as *stimming*. Stimming, for most, appears to be a form of self-soothing, or, just like one attribute of substance abuse, self-medicating. Most people on the autism spectrum have repetitive behaviors to help cope with the uncertainties over daily life, to give structure, and ultimately to help the person with an ASD to relax:

Once in a blue moon, when I have a good, easy day and I feel comfortable, calm, and connected, I'll start to think to myself, "What if I'm not 'really' autistic? I feel pretty normal today!" Then I'll head to the bathroom and dissolve into a compulsive fit of finger waving, or drive home after a day of socializing and screech, squeal, and shriek to myself in my car, and think, "Oh, right. I don't think neurotypical people do this." By now, the only stims I do in public are small, and relatively "normal." I crack my knuckles, bite my lips, hum and whistle, tap my foot or fingers, and clean under my fingernails (instead of biting!). I save my *serious* stimming for private venues. (Lindsmith 2014)

Stimming is not always a means to decompress; one mother of an adult with autism noted that her son "stimmed" when he was happy—similar to an neurotypical individual spontaneously clapping or bouncing when feeling good. In fact, stimming is often seen in the neurotypical world for a variety of reasons. Bouncing a leg up and down when anxious, playing with one's hair, or biting nails. Interestingly, in *Drinking: A Love Story*, Caroline Knapp, the book's presumably neurotypical author, explains how she used to have stimming behaviors as a child:

As soon as I could sit up in my mother's lap, I started rocking, rocking myself back and forth, and I did this for years... I can see the rocking now as a first addiction of sorts. It calmed me, took me out of myself, gave me a sense of relief. I don't know what I needed relief from at that time—age five? Age six?—but I clearly needed relief from something and the rocking worked. I did it daily, sometimes several times a day. I also did it for a long, long time, although when I got old enough to feel self-conscious about it, I kept it secret from everyone: my parents, my sister, my friends. (1997, pp.57–58)

Rocking, an everyday method used to soothe children, is not an uncommon stereotypical behavior for those with autism. Sometimes stereotypic behavior in autism can be seriously self-harming such as head banging. Ghaziuddin (2005) posits that there are two main theories—pain or addiction—to explain why individuals with autism may engage in repetitive self-harming behaviors, and interestingly, both center round the brain's production and release of its own opiates, endorphins (Widmaier, Raff, and Strang 2006). The pain theory suggests that there are significant amounts of the brain's opioids creating a natural analgesic so that the individual does not feel the pain of their behaviors. The addiction theory proposes that the self-injurious behaviors stimulate the brain to produce endorphins, and then the brain becomes addicted and the behaviors persist in order to maintain the brain's opiate production (Ghaziuddin 2005). Interestingly, we find that this self-harming repetitive behavior is an eerie equivalent to the repetition of drug or alcohol abuse in that the immediate rewards offered by drugs and/or alcohol can trump the dire consequences of repeated use. This explains why naltrexone, medication used as a treatment for both opioid and alcohol dependence, has been studied for its effectiveness in treating self-injurious as well as repetitive behaviors in autism, though thus far the studies have shown mixed to minimal results regarding its impact on improving these behaviors (Minshawi *et al.* 2015).

REPETITIVE BEHAVIOR AND SUBSTANCE USE

Szalavitz (2016) notes that the commonality of addiction risk is difficulty with self-regulation. This could mean poor impulse control and acting rash, or high anxiety and behaving cautiously, and in Szalavitz's case, both. Addiction appears to be one way to cope with these particular temperamental traits. Just as stimming and other repetitive behaviors can be a means for those with an ASD to mitigate their anxiety and stress, substance use may not only be misused by an individual for the buzz a particular substance might offer, but also as a repetitive act, where the repetition of using brings with it its own rewards: "Similar brain circuits are involved in both addiction and obsessive-compulsive disorder (OCD): whether the problem is failing to stop an impulsive action or failing to end a habitual routine, many of the same regions are engaged" (Szalavitz 2016, p.62). The similarities between OCD, perseveration, and addiction mean that these habitual behaviors involve impaired regulation. "One critical aspect of addiction, in fact, is an alteration in the balance between brain networks that drive habitual behavior and those that determine whether or not to execute those routines" (Szalavitz 2016, p.63).

ROUTINIZED BEHAVIORS AND AUTISM

Habitual behavior and routines are not necessarily the same as perseveration, but there is some overlap. People with an autism diagnosis may have repetitive behaviors such as stimming to help make order of an unpredictable world, a world that can set someone up for sensory overloads. Perseveration is a means to calm down, but it may or may not coexist with rigid and routinized behaviors, another dominant feature of autism. People often long for structure and can flourish when rigidity and routine are in play. Why the routine? There is a comfort to predictability, especially when the unpredictability of the world can be felt much more intensely by those with autism due to a heightened response to sensual input such as sounds, tastes, textures, etc. Some with autism find that living with the unpredictability of unexpected or unmitigated noises, smells, sensations, or sights to be a huge stressor. Richard Maguire shares his experience, and offers advice for coping with sensory issues.

> Sensory issues will not go away, we have them for life. It is better to deal with them than retreat into a limited life dictated by sensory issues... I carry earplugs or a music player to use in the event of loud noises. I carry a calming stim object... Carry scents that calm you. Wear clothes that are sensory-friendly. Carry dark or colored glasses if they help. The list could go on. (quoted in Attwood et al. 2014, p.109)

When everyday noises or sights might feel like an assault, having predictability makes the world easier to navigate, hence the desire for rigidity or routinized behaviors. It is common for a young child with autism to have a swift and often prolonged meltdown if a routine changes, such as an unexpected change in the drive to school. On The National Autistic Society's website (2016), advice is offered for just this kind of scenario:

> For example, the panic caused by needing to drive a different route to school due to roadworks could trigger a meltdown. In this example, a clear visual support explaining the change, reassurance that the rest of the routine remains the same and adding extra support such as a calming/comforting activity to do in the car could help.

This brings to mind the end of William Faulkner's *The Sound and the Fury* when the character Benjy (Ben), whose diagnosis is left for the reader to decide, is taken on the wrong route home. The description may seem familiar to parents of a child with an ASD:

> For an instant Ben sat in an utter hiatus. Then he bellowed. Bellow on bellow, his voice mounted, with scarce interval for breath. There was more than astonishment in it, it was horror; shock; agony eyeless, tongueless; just sound... Ben's voice mounting toward its unbelievable crescendo...
> "Don't you know any better than to take him to the left?"
> ...Ben's voice roared, and roared. Queenie moved again, her feet began to clop-clop steadily again, and at once Ben hushed. Luster looked quickly back over his shoulder, then he drove on. The broken flower drooped over Ben's fist and his eyes were empty and blue and serene again as cornice and façade flowed smoothly once more from left to right, post and tree, window and doorway and signboard each in its ordered place. (Faulkner 1929, pp.320–321)

ROUTINIZED BEHAVIORS AND SUBSTANCE USE

So how does this relate to substance use? Drinking and drug use can have a scheduled and routinized component. This may seem confusing to those who have witnessed addiction close up; from the outside, the manifestation of an SUD might seem unpredictable and disordered. To many, addiction may not seem to have rules or structure and the repetition of using may seem arbitrary, but, as is often mentioned in substance abuse treatment manuals, "Addicted and compulsive patients have a tendency to adhere rigidly to their ritualist behaviors. For example, those addicted to alcohol will tell you they continue to use the same 'hangouts,' bars and clubs and the same routes to and from those locations" (Kaye, Vadivelu, and Urman 2015, p.374). In Charles Jackson's famous novel of addiction, *The Lost Weekend*, the narrator describes the tumultuous predictability of the (anti)hero's next bender:

> He knew himself well enough also to know that once started, he had to go through it to the end, there was no stopping now, he could not prevent the downward curve to the final state of danger, destruction, or collapse. Short of being locked up, nothing could

help him now till it had played itself out, safely or otherwise. (2013, p.42)

In television, movies, and books, those with addictions are usually characterized as leading isolated, chaotic, and structureless lives in an apparent free-fall that eventually leads them to "hit bottom." But this is not always the case. Those in the substance abuse field often wonder over how some individuals change their behaviors due to a single crisis while others may simply decide they have had enough and "drift out of addiction" (Bischof *et al.* 2003). Robert Cloninger (1987) suggests there are two subgroups of alcoholism: type 1 is associated with traits that might describe an anxious individual—emotionally dependent, cautious, rigid, and orderly; whereas the type 2 subgroup for alcohol misuse is defined as impulsive, uninhibited, and socially detached. It is the former group, type 1, that could line up with an autism diagnosis. Type 1 offers a definition of addiction that can be seen as quite structured and repetitive and loaded with rules. As Szalavitz (2016, p.125) put it:

> ...for someone who finds unstructured social situations uncomfortable, selling, preparing, and/or giving away the drug gave me something specific and ritualized to do...cutting lines with a razor on a mirror—especially chopping up rocks that sparkled like shale or pearl—was also wonderfully satisfying for someone with obsessive tendencies.

Most heroin users know exactly what time each day a dealer will be at a particular spot so they can get their drugs; they will talk about the ritual and pleasure of injecting—and notably, the social benefits of injecting one another (Morris *et al.* 2015). Someone who depends on alcohol may have a particular ritual that is as enjoyable to them as the benefits yielded from the drink itself. When writing about cocaine use, Grund, Ronconi, and Luffa (2013, p.9) share:

> Users adopt rituals, behaviour patterns surrounding substance use, including the methods of acquisition and administration, the selection of the physical and social environment for use, activities after the drug is administered, and methods to prevent unwanted effects of the drug or its status. "Rituals" are influenced by cultural, social and environmental variables, the user is not isolated and the socio-cultural environment is a crucial factor in a social learning process.

Interestingly, many people with SUD are afraid to stop because they fear the loss of the repetition and routine:

> People who are addicted to alcohol or drugs may not hit rock bottom... It may also be that they're comfortable in their addiction, because it is predictable and known. The idea of kicking their habit can be frightening because it involves the unknown. (Horizon Health Services 2014)

This description of the fear of giving up the repetition and routine may sound uncannily familiar to anyone who has a diagnosis of autism or is close to someone with autism.

REPETITIVE NATURE OF GAMING

As mentioned in the previous chapter, gaming and internet use appear to be the addiction most cited for those with an ASD. The repetitive aspect of gaming in particular appears to fit right in with the perseverative and repetitive component of autism: "it [gaming] is easier to manage than real life. It comes with a clear set of rules, structure and repetition" (Grandin and Moore 2015, p.125). When discussing the potential for substance abuse among his clients, the director of a supported employment program for individuals with autism noted that though they have encountered adults in the program who abuse substances, addiction to gaming is far more prevalent. There are individuals who decide they prefer to game all day rather than work: "It's hard for them to recognize boundaries or limits especially with technology invading our workspace. It is harder for our individuals to work on a computer and not game" (Mike Chapman, personal interview, January 17, 2017). Though addiction to gaming is more common among individuals with autism, this does not mean that adults with an ASD are immune to the lure of substance use. This same director went on to describe one client who depended on highly caffeinated beverages such as Red Bull—drinking over 12 in a day— in order to stay awake during the work day as well as sustain his gaming habit late into the night (Mike Chapman, personal interview, January 17, 2017).

DISORGANIZED BEHAVIOR AND DEFICITS IN EXECUTIVE FUNCTIONING

Just as there are subgroups of those diagnosed with alcohol addiction, there are those with autism who can present very differently. This brings us to the impulsive and less routinized individual who may be prone to addiction. This type 2 presents as impetuous, uninhibited, and socially detached, and could describe someone who might have an attention deficit disorder diagnosis. This second type cannot be easily dismissed as not having any relationship to autism since close to one-third of those who receive an autism diagnosis also present with symptoms of ADHD (Rao and Landa 2014).

What is intriguing about autism is that there can be repetitive and routinized behaviors, but at the same time, there is an intensely disorganized and chaotic presentation. Strict rule-following and rigidity can definitely be a protective factor for those with an autism diagnosis.

> When I grew up, I had a rather literal view of addiction, assuming that it would happen immediately, on the first try and that there was no way back. When I was a freshman or sophomore in high school, a girl asked me if I wanted to "get high" with her. I thought she was joking although, in retrospect, I suspect she was almost certainly serious. Otherwise, I was never approached about drugs in high school, possibly because I had a reputation (well deserved) as a severe prude. (Anonymous, self-advocate survey, December 3, 2016)

Another puzzling aspect of an ASD is that rigidity and routine are dominant, and yet, many people with autism are weak at executive functioning, which is the ability to organize and structure one's needs efficiently or, as Lars Perner, an individual with an ASD put it, "One could reasonably say I am highly organized or that I am highly disorganized" (quoted in Attwood *et al.* 2014, p.149). Executive functioning can be compromised so that even though a person with autism may desire a routine and schedule, they will not have the wherewithal to structure their lives to give themselves the routine they desire. This can lead to frustration and in some cases heightened anxiety and depression (Hollocks *et al.* 2014). For example, a person with autism in college may have the ability to focus in and write an excellent paper, but then not know when and where to hand the paper in. So both autism and addiction present with a desire for structure that can eventually be undermined by compromised executive functioning. In *Asperger Syndrome and Alcohol: Drinking to Cope?*, co-author Matt Tinsley described it this way: "My total lack of practicality would have been a recipe for disaster... My problem is in not being able to foresee situations that may arise which require forward planning. This could have led to disaster" (Tinsley and Hendrickx 2008, p.55). Tinsley goes on to note the desire for repetition and poor executive function were both facets of his autism:

> A love of routine and sameness, and reading the same book and watching the same film many, many times was another [symptom of autism]. A total lack of basic common sense was a further symptom which sounded very familiar to me, and had often been the cause of great embarrassment for me... (p.82)

In Tinsley's case, it appears as though both of these characteristics as well as his difficulties in social situations may have led to his addiction to alcohol.

POSITIVES OF PERSEVERATIVE AND REPETITIVE BEHAVIORS IN ASD AND ADDICTION

Of course not all repetitive behaviors lead to negative consequences; there are also ample opportunities for positive outcomes. It is not uncommon for an individual with autism who perseverates on a particular topic to find a way to channel their intense interests to their benefit. Mitch Christian talks of transforming his particular perseverative passion for computers into employment: "My mother used to say that computers were like a surrogate family to me... I think understanding my own skills and interests was key to finding a career path that was suitable for me" (quoted in Attwood *et al.* 2014, p.217). Others can achieve social inclusion by sharing their interests via groups, chatrooms, and clubs of like-minded individuals. In *Neurotribes*, Silberman (2015) shares the story of the eighteenth-century philosopher Henry Cavendish (posthumously diagnosed with Asperger's Syndrome by the neurologist Oliver Sacks) who was described during and after his lifetime as a social enigma. Cavendish would perseverate on particular scientific experiments leading to significant discoveries. His special interests allowed him opportunities to connect on his terms with other like-minded individuals in scientific societies.

Interestingly, repetitive and routinized behaviors can be an asset when trying to overcome an addiction. For example, Tinsley (Tinsley and Hendrickt 2008, p.95) shares how routine and repetitions helped in his recovery:

> The first thing I discovered was that there was a fixed routine for attending groups and doing tasks such as housework and shopping... I have brought this structure into my new life after rehab, having weekly schedules pinned up by my bed, so that I always have a picture in my mind of the days ahead. This approach helps to manage the need for predictability and structure that many with AS find so important. (p.95)

Rengit *et al.* (2016) suggest tapping into the desire for routine by incorporating a "goal tracking" or "monitoring log" so that their patient (who had both autism and a substance use diagnosis) could keep track of his diminishing substance use. They found this patient liked the data and the "ritual of tracking." Indeed, it could be an effective and productive strategy for clinicians, family, and self-advocates who have both an ASD and SUD to tap into the desire for routine and repetition, and redirect it to help diminish substance use and maintain recovery.

CHAPTER 4

GENETIC PREDISPOSITIONS AND CONNECTIONS

The genetic connections regarding autism and substance abuse can be as tangled and interconnected as our genes and their mutations appear to be. Both autism and a substance use diagnosis have clear and significant genetic components, but there is still a great deal of uncertainty regarding the association between genetic influences and environmental impacts. At the time we wrote this chapter (and studies continue to emerge at a rapid pace), the literature clearly supports the thesis that autism has a significant genetic component, with current findings suggesting there is a 74–98 percent heritability rate (Entine and Locwin 2016). SUD also has a genetic component that appears to be less significant than ASD, which makes sense given that environmental factors play a greater role in the diagnosis of SUD than a diagnosis of ASD. Of course, acknowledging the importance of the environmental impact on getting an SUD makes a lot of sense since one cannot have an SUD without having been introduced to a substance. There is also the added complication of what substance is being abused and its particular impact on the body chemistry. Still, both an ASD and SUD have genetic components, and it appears that some of these components may overlap.

TWIN STUDIES: NATURE VERSUS NURTURE

When exploring the literature of certain disorders and diseases, it is clear that our genes are implicated, but what is unclear is how other non-genetic factors can influence them. We are all born with certain genes that carry certain DNA that affect how we look and act. Medically, our genes can also impact our susceptibility to disease and disorders. Essentially, a genotype is the identity we inherit, a set of instructions for the development and maintenance of our bodies. A phenotype is the physical presentation of our genotype: eye color, texture of our hair, height, and so on. A phenotype also describes our behaviors and manner, whether we are seen as anxious and thin, jovial and rotund, or a myriad of other physical and emotional combinations. These blends of physical features and temperaments are not all heritable; a person may be anxious around dogs, but that may be the result of a bad childhood experience with dogs. The genotype may express that an individual might have more anxiety, but environmental exposure to a dog at a young age created the phenotype that is a particular person's *dogphobia*. This is what is meant by *nature versus nurture*, the impact of the environment on one's personal genome known as epigenetics (Personal Genetics Education Project 2017).

Epigenetics is the intersection of science and social science, and is directly related to autism and addiction. Epigenetic flags are responsible for turning on or off certain genes. So, though one may carry a particular genetic code, it is not a forgone conclusion that a particular gene will be expressed. This is why twin studies are so popular in research. Initially identical twins share the same genome and epigenomes and yet, identical twins (or monozygotic twins) can each turn out differently—which allows researchers to speculate over what to attribute to nature and what to attribute to nurture. To put the problem another way, current research is investigating biological factors in conjunction with environmental factors. What becomes tricky when looking at genetic research is that some of the epigenetic tags that allow for genes to be expressed or suppressed develop as we develop, and may or may not pass on to the next generation. This makes it difficult to tease out if a mutated gene is solely responsible for developing a disease or disorder. So, though twins have exactly the same DNA (with exactly the same epigenetic flags, initially), those epigenetic markers may not develop identically as the twins age. For example, if one twin gets a lot of exercise while another does not, or if one twin has a more stressful job than the other, their genetic expression can change, and the two may no longer have identical genetic expression, even if their DNA is fundamentally identical (Genetic Science Learning Center 2013).

Another type of twin study is one that compares monozygotic (MZ), or identical, twins, and dizygotic (DZ), or fraternal, twins. These studies are particularly effective because, for the most part, the controls (same age, same family, same environments) are built in, and the only major difference between these two twin types is that MZ twins share identical DNA while DZ twins do not. If a study involving both MZ and DZ twins proves that MZ twins have a higher *concordance rate* (that is, a trait that is present in both individuals in that twin set) compared to the DZ twins, there is clearly a genetic component, since an environmental impact would most likely be the same for both identical and fraternal twins (MSU Twin Registry 2017).

This nurture vs. nature element of genetic expression can easily identify particular disorders as having more or less environmental components. When looking at what might influence an autism or addiction diagnosis, it is not surprising that there is more evidence of a genetic link with autism than addiction. Both diagnoses have a large genetic component, but how that component is expressed is different. In the case of autism, the outside environmental impacts are as yet unknown. Some speculate that vaccines and diets may cause autism, but recent research, including brain scans of infants, debunks those theories (Callaway 2017). It appears that the environmental factors that contribute to an autism diagnosis were introduced to the parents prior to conception, or while the child was in utero.

The diagnosis of an SUD is different from other mental health diagnoses in that it requires the individual to engage in a specific behavior (that is, using the substance) in order to develop the condition. One may be genetically susceptible to addiction, but genetic susceptibility alone is not sufficient for development of the condition; the individual must be exposed to the substance (Joseph Williams, personal communication, April 27, 2017). One might know that addiction runs in the family and suspect a significant genetic predisposition for addiction but may never know if an SUD would emerge if alcohol or drugs are not introduced. It is the act of choosing to use drugs that gives addiction the moral and punitive overlay that few other diagnoses share. There are many environmental and personal factors (temperament, trauma, stress, peer pressure, etc.) that could lead an individual to use mind-altering substances and possibly develop an addiction. This is why the recent opioid epidemic has changed the tenor of anti-drug rhetoric in recent years. Prescription opioid use has played a major role in the current addiction crisis in this country. In this case, the medical community bears some responsibility in exposing significant numbers of individuals who may have a genetic predisposition for addiction to substances that can then lead to the development of an SUD (Joseph Williams, personal communication, April 27, 2017). As such, the rise in prescription drug and heroin addiction is, in part, an iatrogenic event (that is, one caused or precipitated by a medical treatment). It is harder to blame the person with the addiction if it was their healthcare provider who instigated it, and one result is a remarkable change in tone toward substance abuse. We might hope that this less punitive approach could reduce the stigma that is associated with an SUD. After all, addiction is partially a genetic disorder no different from a host of other genetic disorders; it just needs that second hit of substance use to activate it. Although there are common genes that might make individuals susceptible to addiction, it is not helpful to stigmatize the use of alcohol or different types of drugs since each substance appears to have its own particular relationship to our DNA. "Genetic factors exist that are both specific to certain individual drugs of abuse, including stimulants, and general to multiple forms of abuse or dependence" (Galanter, Kleber, and Brady 2014, p.27).

COMORBIDITY WITH ASD

In previous chapters we referred to other mental health diagnoses that are often concurrent with an autism diagnosis. Depression, ADHD, and anxiety are the most common co-diagnoses or, to use a word often employed by mental health/disabilities professionals, *comorbidities.* It is suggested that 65–80 percent of individuals with an autism diagnosis also have a coexisting psychiatric disorder (de Bruin *et al.* 2007; Ghaziuddin *et al.* 1998; Leyfer *et al.* 2006; Sterling *et al.* 2008). Such high numbers would indicate a genetic predisposition to those disorders. There are numerous genetic studies linking ASD to depression, anxiety, and ADHD, but recently there have also been studies that indicate there is a common genetic variant among less linked diagnoses. Researchers such as Bates (2013, p.1) have noted, "We have been able to discover specific genetic variants that seem to overlap among disorders that we think of as very clinically different." Although these other mental health diagnoses, including substance use, have not, until recently, been linked to autism, the fact that they may have a common genetic root could mean that there are certain underlying similarities that, prior to this genetic research, have been discounted (Bates 2013). Although the commonality of certain genes in seemingly unrelated conditions may appear to make the diagnostic landscape a little hazier, ultimately it proves postulations that have been suspected for quite some time regarding autism, that there is not a single gene that is responsible. Instead, there appear to be "many different underlying physical and genetic factors" (Bates 2013, p.1). Why are these connections important? Not only could this genetic research provide answers as to why people develop different mental health diagnoses, but the findings might also lead to new and possibly unexpected treatments.

SUBSTANCE USE AND AUTISM

Just as it may be true of autism, this complex and multi-factored genetic presentation may also be true of SUD. As noted earlier, there doesn't seem to be one specific explanation as to why two siblings with similar genetic make-up might have very different relationships to their substance intake and dependence. There is one factor that separates the genetic predisposition to substance abuse from other genetically predetermined conditions. As mentioned earlier in this chapter, in the case of SUD, there is a necessary environmental component—a substance *must* be introduced in order to develop an addiction to it (Gelernter *et al.* 2014). An environmental component may not be involved with autism since, as far as we know (despite controversy regarding vaccines and diets), currently no specific environmental factor has been uncovered that might activate autism. In the case of SUD, clearly different genetic make-ups metabolize particular substances in distinct ways. Anecdotally, individuals not prone to addiction often struggle to understand why another might succumb to drugs or alcohol. As Andrew Solomon (2001, p.223) put it: "People who claim not to understand why anyone would get addicted to drugs are usually people who haven't tried them or who are genetically fairly invulnerable to them." For example, the difference in responses to Question 3, "What effect does alcohol have on you, particularly on your executive function or stimming?", from Musings of an Aspie blog's "How We Experience the World Survey":

I left quite a large, and loud, group of friends/acquaintances in Ireland (I'm now in US), and I suspect it will be the last time I ever have that. It's too much for me, and involved way too much alcohol to cope, to fit in. Sadly, the stereotype of how much Irish people drink tends to hold true for many. I will do my best to keep the three or four very dear individual friends I have, however. I would guess that they all veer towards NT, but I am drawn towards rule-breakers, to people who do not neatly fit their surroundings, so they accept me as I am, and accept how, and when, I choose to communicate...

Alcohol is not my friend. I do enjoy a glass or two of wine but if I overindulge slightly I feel like someone has beaten me with a baseball bat, my skin hurts. (Kim, July 14, 2014)

As noted earlier in this book, people with an ASD may well feel misunderstood by the neurotypical population, yet no one would accuse someone with autism of choosing to have an ASD. The same is not true for those with addictions. If one is not genetically predisposed to enjoy alcohol or drugs and feel the benefits, one may not have the compassion to understand the draw of illicit substances and why people they know and love might become addicted. As one person with an ASD shared on our self-advocate survey regarding their drug and alcohol use, "Drugs are bad for you. I have not been around people drunk or on drugs" (Anonymous, self-advocate survey, December 5, 2016).

GENETIC LINK BETWEEN ASD AND SUD

Is there a genetic link between ASD and SUD? Now that genetic researchers have expanded their investigations into fields that may previously have seemed disconnected, the answer seems to be, maybe. Certain studies do point to a genetic link between the two (Butwicka *et al.* 2017; Chen *et al.* 2013; Rothwell 2016). For example, although many gene mutations have been associated with autism, recent studies have found specific genes prevalent in those with an autism diagnosis that also impact addiction. One gene associated with autism, named *AUTS2* (autism susceptibility candidate 2) (SFARI 2016), has been shown to be connected to both alcohol and heroin consumption (Chen *et al.* 2013; Schumann *et al.* 2011). This is not to say that those who have this genetic variant will be diagnosed with both autism and addiction, but it does mean that this same gene is related to both diagnoses. It is unclear what these associations might yield for the future, but it is reasonable to predict that connecting the dots could offer more targeted and effective management of both disorders.

But the point of discussing genetics in relation to ASD and SUD is not so much finding genetic connections between the two, but instead, understanding the importance of genetic predisposition and characteristics that could impact our view of both diagnoses and how to go about treating them. As we already know, the discovery of a gene that may cause an illness or a disorder does not necessarily lead to curing said illness or disorder. For example, in 1993 researchers discovered that changes in the *HTT* gene were the cause of Huntington's disease, a known heritable condition that attacks certain parts of the brain and is ultimately fatal. The discovery of this gene has had a huge impact on the Huntington's community, resulting in a genetic test to let individuals at risk know if they would or would not develop Huntington's, and it also gave carriers the ability to make informed decisions and choices if they were planning on having children. On top of offering the Huntington's community the opportunity to get a clearer picture of their futures, there was also an expectation that now, with the gene isolated, it could possibly be targeted, hope rose for a cure. Almost 25 years after discovering *HTT* there is still no cure for Huntington's disease. It turns out that the gene hosts alleles (one or more variant forms of a gene, found at the same place on a chromosome, that arise by mutation) that can create tangled and thorny connections that bind and attach with other genes in such a way that the alleles cannot be easily teased apart. And even if the gene could be isolated and eradicated, tampering with genetics in such a way raises a host of ethical issues that range from the temptation to make designer babies to inadvertently creating new diseases or disorders (National Academy of Science and the National Academy of Medicine 2017). This is to say that currently, genetic research can offer invaluable information and in some instances treatment, but it is not a panacea.

HOW GENETIC RESEARCH CAN HELP IN TREATMENT
What genetic research has offered thus far is a much fuller understanding of particular conditions. Genetic studies will no doubt continue to spur on a variety of unexpected and fruitful connections. In the case of ASD, researchers can now alter the genes in mice so that they carry certain autism-specific mutations for the study of explicit aspects of

brain function. This will allow them to get a better understanding of the impact of a particular gene on the brain and body. Their research could ultimately create targeted therapeutic interventions (Jeste and Geschwind 2014). In the previous chapters we discussed the connections between repetitive behaviors and social anxiety, and their connections to both autism and SUDs. Neuroscientists can now study the brains of mice with particular genes associated with specific disorders in order to find what pathways and receptors in the brain respond to targeted stimuli and map a disorder's hallmark actions or emotions.

Now that behavioral commonalities between autism and substance abuse are coming to the fore, genetic research can have a significant impact on both (de Alwis *et al.* 2014). For instance, there have been a number of studies targeting oxytocin, a natural hormone that regulates social bonding, maternal behaviors, and sexual pleasure neurotransmissions in the brain. The research regarding the oxytocin hormone is an example of how particular genetic studies can have an impact on both ASD and SUD. Researchers noticed that mice bred with a mutation in a gene associated with autism had less oxytocin in their brains than typical mice (Peñagarikano *et al.* 2015). Oxytocin is now being tested as a possible treatment for social and cognitive impairments that go along with a variety of diagnoses including autism and addiction (DeAngelis 2008; Kovács, Sarnyai, and Szabó 1998; McGregor and Bowen 2012; Young and Barrett 2015). There has been a surge of studies in the ASD and SUD fields targeting oxytocin. Why autism and substance use? Research focusing on those with ASD indicates that oxytocin might improve social function and empathy (Anagnostou *et al.* 2014). Studies suggest that some individuals with a diagnosis of autism have a variant in the oxytocin receptor gene that could impact social bonding (LoParo and Waldman 2015). Research indicates that something similar may impact the brains of individuals with an SUD, affecting their social connections and making them more vulnerable to seek pleasure through drugs, since social bonding offers minimal rewards (Szalavitz 2017). There is also evidence that the prosocial aspects of a drug like Ecstasy might be due to the stimulation of the brain's oxytocin systems (Dumont *et al.* 2009). Moreover, studies indicate, "oxytocin clearly has acute inhibitory effects on the intake of alcohol, opiates and stimulants" (McGregor and Bowen 2012, p.336). Although it is not at all clear if oxytocin regulation would be an appropriate treatment for either ASD or SUD, it is one of many neurobiological options currently being investigated. Other research studies indicate there are commonalities in neurological pathways, receptors, and molecules that regulate dopamine, endorphins, endcocannabinoids that appear to be related to both autism and addiction, and could potentially provide links between the two (Rothwell 2016).

This recent surge of neurobiological research offers exciting opportunities to rethink how a person's genetic make-up could not only determine an ASD, SUD, or a number of other diagnoses, but could also potentially regulate how an individual may respond to treatments. It also leads researchers to expand their approach to not just looking at the disorder in front of them, but exploring the connections among diagnoses. Given that those with an SUD or ASD are prone to a variety of comorbidities, especially depression, anxiety, and ADHD, it makes sense that finding genetic connections and commonalities might bolster outcomes.

GEEK SYNDROME

Speculation regarding genetics has raised a variety of interesting questions and theories related to natural selection and genetic adaptation. In 2001 Steve Silberman wrote a provocative article for *Wired* titled "The Geek Syndrome." The article explored whether breeding among individuals with autism or autistic traits could partly explain the rise in the numbers of individuals being diagnosed with autism. Essentially, the hypothesis was evolutionary: individuals with autism or autistic traits such as engineers and mathematicians were, due to the digital revolution, in great demand in places such as Silicon Valley:

> It's a familiar joke in the industry that many of the hardcore programmers in IT strongholds like Intel, Adobe, and Silicon Graphics—coming to work early, leaving late, sucking down Big Gulps in their cubicles while they code for hours—are residing somewhere in Asperger's domain. (Silberman 2001)

In the past, many of these individuals might have worked in more solitary quarters, but, according to Silberman, the tech boom created an environment where these *techies* were in close quarters where they met, socialized, and began procreating. Essentially Silberman's article allowed for theories that the rise in autism diagnoses could be a direct consequence of the digital revolution. According to the article, the outcome of Geek Syndrome was an increase of children with autism and autistic traits. This hypothesis has some merit, as seen in Roelfsema *et al.*'s 2012 study comparing autism rates in towns that do and do not have high levels of information technology workers. As a colleague in the field noted:

> ...49% of the gene variants that cause autism are thought to exist commonly in the whole human population. The hypothesis is that when a few of these variants are in one individual they do not cause ASD but when many of them are, they cause ASD. Therefore it would make sense that when two geeks (who are geeks because they have a few of these variants!) get together, they have a kid with a combination of these variants kicking over the threshold and they have autism. This accounts for the broader autism phenotype... (Personal communication, April 28, 2017)

Given these hypotheses and studies, the leap could be made that in the twenty-first century, with the dominance of technology, there is speculation that the spike in autism diagnoses might be evolutionary, an illustration of Darwin's hypothesis of *survival of the fittest*. A more reasonable explanation of the rise of ASD in certain tech-heavy communities is *gene flow*. This is the transfer of alleles from one population to another. The rise in technology brought people together who might not otherwise have met, and they effectively "cross pollinate." This is illustrated by the prevalence of individuals with autistic features during the tech boom.

> The lone-wolf programmer may be the research director of a major company, managing the back end of an IT empire at a comfortable remove from the actual clients. Says Bryna Siegel, author of *The World of the Autistic Child* and director of the PDD clinic at UCSF. In another historical time, these men would have become monks, developing new ink for early printing presses. Suddenly they're making $150,000 a year with stock options. They're reproducing at a much higher rate. (Silberman 2001)

It is true that the "nerd" or "geek," once an object of ridicule in popular culture, now retains an elevated social status. For example, 30 years ago, adults interested in comic books and action heroes who might have only found company, safety, and solace in cramped comic book shops may now openly gather in multiplexes to watch the latest in a string of movies based on comic book heroes, or "cosplay" by the thousands in spacious convention centers. Those who were once ostracized for being nerds are now in the mainstream:

> But as recently as two to three decades ago, kids on the spectrum were mercilessly teased as being nerds or geeks. While many today wear those labels as points of pride, it was certainly not the case back then—they were used as put-downs, a way of calling out kids who had a hard time socializing—and who at the same time exhibited a kind of smartness that caused them to be alienated from the "normal" kids. (Dvorsky 2012)

The risk of recognizing a theory like Geek Syndrome is that it is essentially aimed to reflect one end of the autism spectrum. Indeed, in a 2013 study exploring the evolutionary survival of certain mental health diagnoses, Power *et al.* found that there appears to be a strong negative selection among those with genetic links to autism. This means that those with autism and their siblings have fewer children than the general population. Given the heritability of autism, this study goes against the anecdotal evidence provided in the Geek Syndrome. Interestingly, this same study found that there was an average to higher rate of reproduction among the siblings of those with an SUD. But given the environmental component of SUDs mentioned earlier, combined with the uneven outcomes of groups from different cultural backgrounds and their ability to metabolize drugs and alcohol, there are far too many variables to offer a definitive explanation for this result.

Whether evolutionary forces are at work or not, the current studies pointing to a higher rate of addiction for those with ASD than the general population (Butwicka *et al.* 2017) combined with the strong genetic connections between an autism and substance use diagnoses suggest the need for continued research exploring the connections between the two. Research aimed at the common biological factors of SUD and ASD might be able to offer the opportunity to compose accurate and targeted assessments and treatments for both populations.

CHAPTER 5

LATE DIAGNOSIS AND ITS CONNECTION TO SUBSTANCE USE

As we researched forums, memoirs, studies, and other sources for this book, it became clear to us that there was a common thread: many of the individuals who disclosed having a dual diagnosis of a substance use diagnosis and an autism spectrum diagnosis had received a late diagnosis of autism in adulthood. This particular fact seemed noteworthy in that it raised several questions—can the higher rates of SUD among those with an ASD be attributed to undiagnosed or misdiagnosed teenagers and adults using substances to self-medicate? Does having an official diagnosis of autism lead to better outcomes? Could early diagnosis and appropriate treatment be a protective factor? If so, does this mean that the rates of addiction among those with autism will drop significantly in the next few years (now that more individuals diagnosed as children are reaching adulthood)?

Given how little research there appears to be regarding the outcomes of adults with a late diagnosis of autism versus those who grew up knowing they had an ASD, it is hard to answer definitively the questions posed above, but it is possible to speculate. Much of the literature regarding substance use and autism implies that many of the individual cases cited were using drugs or alcohol to self-medicate. "I liked it [alcohol] from the start—the tingling sense of permission it gave, the enhanced conviviality, the diminution of self-consciousness, and the temporary immunity from the personal demons that it provided..." (Page 2009, p.109). Individuals with an ASD claim that the struggle of always knowing they were different, unable to meet expectations, living in an unsafe, unpredictable world, feeling socially awkward and alienated, led them to abuse substances:

> In essence, alcohol made Matt "normal". He has spoken of being puzzled at this time as to why everyone else wasn't as drunk as he was. He had mistakenly assumed that others were experiencing the same levels of anxiety as he was and would feel equal joy at finding release from this. (Tinsley and Hendrickx 2008, p.42)

Would someone who was aware of their autism diagnosis from childhood feel the same way as adult-diagnosed Matt?

Philip Wylie, in his book about late ASD, shares a list of his epiphanies after receiving his Asperger's diagnosis in his fifties:

> Now I understood why I had always had relationship problems both inside and outside my family. It explained to some extent why I was constructively dismissed by the firm of accountants for which I had worked. It also made sense of the fact that so many people had described me as being strange, eccentric, interesting, ungrounded, uncoordinated, selfish and so forth. (Wylie 2014, p.20)

These are the words of a man who was diagnosed at the age of 52, but interestingly, Wylie's words do not seem much different from those posted by a college student who received his Asperger's Syndrome diagnosis as a child:

> I became more withdrawn, and began to feel "ashamed" of how I was and how I was getting along with the other students. Even more frustrating was the feeling that I couldn't tell anyone about it, and that I would give everyone a misguided impression of who I really was.
>
> I was a person who loved the time he had to himself, to escape into the world of comic books, history and studying language for fun. But as I was a volunteer, I had to interact with others during the day, and I had to participate in the "bonding activities" meant to bring us together.
>
> With each passing day, I learned how strange I felt, how separate I felt, and I started to feel like I could not keep these emotions within me for any longer. (Silva 2015)

PROTECTIVE FACTORS OF AN EARLY DIAGNOSIS

If, as researchers have speculated, individuals use substances such as alcohol or drugs to deal with living with undiagnosed autism (Clarke *et al.* 2016; Tinsley and Hendrickx 2008), what might that mean for those with an early diagnosis sharing the same underlying issues? Given the dearth of literature comparing the outcomes of those with an early diagnosis of autism with those diagnosed in adulthood, one way to compare the two would be to look at the protective and risk factors associated with each diagnosis. The hope is that digging deeper into the possible differences and similarities might offer some insight into whether an early or late diagnosis could put an individual at risk for a co-occurring SUD.

For the past 20 years, early diagnosis and treatment has been the rallying cry within the autism community. Studies show that early intervention improves the child's global development. Many of the issues noted earlier in this book, such as sensory regulation, social skills, and adaptation to new and unexpected environments, can be greatly improved by autism-specific therapies targeted to both the parents and children. Recently, applied behavioral analysis (ABA) has received a great deal of positive press for "curing" autism (Padawer 2014). The findings of studies sited in the article by Orinstein *et al.* (2014) and Anderson, Liang, and Lord (2014) found that a handful of their patients who received ABA for several years had shed the hallmark characteristics of autism and were indistinguishable from their neurotypical peers. Of course, these findings have stirred much controversy. Many self-advocates see their autism as an asset and do not find neurotypicality as a goal worth striving for:

> Someone once asked me if I would take a "cure" for my autism if there was one. I said "No." I am not sick, I don't need medicine for my autism. Suggesting I need to be cured implies I'm not OK with being autistic. It also implies that being typical is superior and it's not. I know many typical individuals who live with a variety of difficulties and these go with being human. If I were born with a typical brain it does not mean I'm immune to problems. So, being typical will not fix me, because I'm not broken. (Wylie, Lawson, and Beardon 2016, p.141)

The ABA *optimal outcomes* also provoked wary warnings from practitioners anxious to remind caregivers that this "cure" had an impact on a tiny fraction of the autism population who received ABA and/or other treatments. In the case of optimal outcomes and their relationship to addictions, the Orinstein *et al.* (2014) study reports a decline in the comorbidity rates of ADHD, anxiety, and depression for these particular individuals as they aged. If this early intervention can offer a reduction in autism symptoms and a decline in other mental health diagnoses, then those who respond well do prove, in these specific cases, that early intervention could be a protective factor for substance use. But *optimal outcomes* are not the norm. According to the studies, only 9 percent of individuals with autism had an optimal outcome to treatment. Though 9 percent is statistically significant, the vast majority of those receiving treatment after an early diagnosis are still struggling with symptoms of autism.

Earlier in this book we noted that families of individuals with ASD and the professionals working with them appear to find that many of the symptoms of ASD are inherent protective factors against substance abuse. Limited social skills, sensory sensitivities, rigidity, and rule-following are all examples of why an individual with autism would not succumb to an SUD. For example, one parent responding to a survey for this book noted:

> My son is 10, so he hasn't had the opportunity to get drugs or alcohol; however, he is also extremely health conscious (hypochondria) and has an anxiety disorder. He won't even touch unlit cigarettes or empty wine bottles for fear they might harm him—I doubt he would ever use drugs/alcohol if given the opportunity. (Anonymous, family member survey, December 15, 2016)

What is heartening about this quote is not the assumed protective factors offered by the symptoms of autism such as anxiety and rule-following (Ramos *et al.* 2013), since those assumptions could dissipate as the child ages (Butwicka *et al.* 2017). What bodes well for this particular child is the parent is in close proximity, listening to what the child has to say, and paying attention to him. Vigilance and involvement on the part of caregivers is definitely an asset when it comes to substance use (Office of the Surgeon General 2016). Children with an early diagnosis may have an advantage in that, in most cases, one or more of their caregivers is paying attention to their child and having them seen by a professional. These early diagnosed children also have schools and other institutions willing to make accommodations so that they can have a much better chance of academic and social success, as can be seen from the Autism Speaks' "Educating Students with Autism" flyer:

> Educating students with autism is usually an intensive undertaking, involving a team of professionals and many hours each week of different instruction and therapies to address a student's behavioral, developmental, social and/or academic needs. Students with autism often require explicit teaching across a variety of settings to generalize skills. (2012, p.74)

Identifying autism at an early age appears to offer huge advantages, particularly in school, compared to someone who remained undiagnosed in school:

> ...my father was incredulous that a boy who blithely recited the names and dates of all the United States' presidents and their wives in order (backward upon request) couldn't manage to pass elementary math and science. My grades only worsened as teachers expected more of me. (Page 2009, p.38)

EARLY DIAGNOSIS AND ADVOCACY

Another protective factor for those diagnosed when young (if all goes well in the family, schools, and community) is that they are accustomed to getting help and being offered modifications, and may be more likely to advocate for themselves and seek help when necessary. One educator who works for a college program specifically geared toward individuals with autism shared that the students who grew up knowing they had an autism diagnosis seemed more comfortable in the program, were better able to assess their strengths and deficits, and were much more at ease asking for assistance than their classmates who were diagnosed in their teens (Vannee Cao-Nguyen, personal interview, February 24, 2017).

And asking for help and being comfortable with one's diagnosis is a huge advantage for an individual with autism. It is encouraging to see children being raised knowing they have autism and feeling natural and comfortable enough to own and take pride in that diagnosis. Disability rights advocates have worked hard to steer family and community to not stigmatize or see shame in a child's differences.

Being raised by advocates could allow a child with an ASD to be comfortable in their own skin:

> mum explained to me that i was wired differently, that it wasn't a bad thing, She said that i could just do things differently but i would still get everything done. And that was called Aspergers!
>
> i learned to enjoy my Aspergers. (AutisticandProud January 31, 2013)

When transitioning into post-secondary educational settings, Camarena and Sarigiani (2009) suggest there were better outcomes for adolescents who understood and accepted their autism diagnosis than those who did not.

Another influential positive outcome associated with early diagnosis and intervention is its huge impact on autism awareness. When an adult receives an autism diagnosis, they may have already become isolated and burned many bridges by frustrating their family and community due to their differences. The advent of improved childhood screenings and early diagnoses unleashed the power of parents of all backgrounds, educational levels, and other diverse demographics to come together to rally and advocate for their children. This has had a significant impact on services, research, and treatment, and has created an atmosphere of acceptance and tolerance toward those with autism. Comparatively, communities associated with late onset illnesses such as schizophrenia, borderline personality disorder, or a substance use diagnosis do not get the same treatment. The parents of children with late onset illnesses might be distanced or completely alienated by the time their child gets the proper diagnosis; their child may no longer seem sweet or innocent but instead come across as frightening or duplicitous. It may be much harder to mine their own compassion let alone advocate for the compassion, support, and tolerance of others. Early identification has unleashed a level of disabilities activism that makes 24-hour telethons and other outreach undertakings of the past seem ineffective and quaint.

EARLY DIAGNOSIS IS NOT EQUAL FOR ALL

Yet, despite all the publicity and activism, there is still an array of racial, cultural, economic, and social implications associated with early diagnosis and treatment. For instance, in one study of children's first specialty care visits, white children were 2.6 times more likely to be diagnosed with an ASD than African-American children, while African-American children were five times more likely to receive an ADHD diagnosis than their white cohorts (Mandell *et al.* 2007). Studies like this do not imply genetic predispositions of one group over another, but rather, racial bias by the professionals conducting the assessments. So, though early diagnosis may offer the advantage of more parental involvement and monitoring, it is unclear if that advantage is undermined by a system that may not offer proper diagnoses, services, and treatments to particular populations. An early diagnosis should offer the support of seasoned, thoughtful professionals and caring family and community members, but along with that there is often the underlying assumption that a family will have the economic wherewithal to ensure the child gets all they need:

> There were many therapies that we wanted to try, but had to skip because we simply couldn't afford them. We wanted to get Davis more speech therapy, some socialization classes, the list goes on and on. It might have helped, but we had to be realistic about our finances. (Nguyen 2013)

There is also the assumption that the parent can spend significant time with their child, and the child's school will have the resources to take note of a child's stressors and reactions in order to offer assistance and aid. All these supports are protective factors for preventing SUD (Beyers *et al.* 2004; Hawkins, Catalano, and Arthur 2002). The question is, does the child who receives an early diagnosis of autism have access to these services and supports that would lead to better outcomes? And even if the child is receiving services after their early diagnosis, does every family truly benefit from an early diagnosis in the long term?

EARLY DIAGNOSIS OF ASD AS A RISK FACTOR

These questions highlight some of the risk factors of an early diagnosis. Early intervention is presented to parents as their best option for a better life for them and for their child. It is clear that early intervention is critical, particularly for academic success, but there can be downsides to receiving an early diagnosis that should be addressed. Quality early intervention, for many, is not inexpensive; most parents who have a child with autism become financially and emotionally stressed by the task of getting assistance for their child (Tehee, Honan, and Hevey 2009). Parents regularly reduce their working hours or take lower-pressure, lower-paying jobs so that they can be available to their children and accommodate what can often be a particularly challenging schedule of treatments and therapies. Often by the time the child becomes an adolescent, parents and siblings are maxed out, emotionally and financially. In a study of parental stressors, one parent shared, "Non-reimbursed therapies and equipment put strain on family budget. Other family members need counseling and medication to cope with the stress of living with autistic child. These costs further strain family budget" (quoted in Sharpe and Baker 2007, p.259). These stressors may not only have a negative impact on the families of those with ASD, but they also have an impact on the family member who has an autism diagnosis (Meadan, Halle, and Ebata 2010). On top of this, despite the optimal outcomes for a handful of individuals, the statistics still show poor adult success rates, regardless of when they received a diagnosis and what treatment they may have received (Howlin *et al.* 2004; Scott *et al.* 2015).

Even when an individual has had the appropriate early interventions and the outcomes of those interventions are successful, long-term outcomes cannot be guaranteed. An educationally mainstreamed child may maintain or develop the social awkwardness and pressures, the co-occurring anxieties and depressions, and the constant need to accommodate sensory stressors that are risk factors for an adolescent/ adult with autism:

> I thankfully wasn't bullied which was probably a very, I'd say lucky. I was slightly bullied on my paper round, but not actually in school, so it wasn't bad. But the big change, the big change came when I was about 15. My ability to cope for some reason, just simply declined pretty quickly. I think it was the level of stress I was under at school, quite simply. (HealthTalk July 2016)

The underlying expectations that a person with autism who has received and responded to early treatment can integrate effortlessly into adolescent life despite not having shed all the various facets of autism may put an adolescent or young adult at risk of developing an SUD.

What might be seen as a protective factor can also be seen as a risk factor. The fact that those diagnosed young might be used to receiving treatment and therefore more willing to ask for help when older could backfire. First, some adolescents who have had involved family members and resource teachers advocate for them over the years may not have acquired effective self-advocacy skills as others have been advocating on their behalf (Camarena and Sarigiani 2009). In post-secondary educational settings this can be dangerous, putting the college student with an autism diagnosis at risk for academic and possibly social failures. Given the sudden deluge of literature addressing the transition process for individuals with an ASD enrolling in college, it is striking that there is hardly any mention of drugs or alcohol. In a search of the literature evaluating the potential needs of ASD students transitioning to college, the only reference to alcohol was a possible response of students with an ASD to their neurotypical peers: "…they [students with ASD] may become anxious or agitated when other students break an established rule (e.g., the honor policy for test taking, no alcohol rules in the dorm) and may attempt to enforce the rules on their own" (Adreon and Durocher 2007, p.273). Interestingly one of the few references to drugs and alcohol was in a 2016 *New York Times* article reporting on the "first generation of college students with an autism diagnosis" (Hoffman 2016). In it, Hoffman briefly alludes to reasons ASD students don't succeed: "Some crumble under academic and organizational stress. Others succumb to campus allures like alcohol and drugs" (Hoffman 2016).

College is not the only route for adults raised with the knowledge that they are on the spectrum. Services for adults with ASD are not as plentiful and well funded as early intervention services. Unlike a public school that is required to accept local students and abide by the Individuals with Disabilities Education Act (IDEA), employers can find reasons to skirt the Americans with Disabilities Act (ADA) simply by not hiring individuals with disabilities. People with autism often cannot make it past the initial interview due to seeming odd or antisocial. Debbie Denneburg recalls one of her botched job interviews: "'Because I need to eat!' That is the response I gave a potential employer when they asked me why I wanted to work for them. Although it was the truth, it was the wrong answer" (quoted in

Attwood *et al.* 2014, p.215). Workplaces that do hire individuals with ASD are expected to make reasonable accommodations but, unlike schools that might allow a student extra time on a test, or offer to separate a student from the rest of the class when a group activity is too overwhelming, workplaces do not, and fiscally cannot, make these adaptations. A small business may not be able to afford to make the accommodations for, say, *organization and prioritization,* one of several categories that a business may have to consider when hiring someone with an autism diagnosis:

> **Organization and Prioritization:** Individuals with ASD may have difficulty getting or staying organized, or have difficulty prioritizing tasks at work. The employee may need assistance with skills required to prepare and execute complex behavior like planning, goal setting, and task completion.
>
> Practical Solutions • Workplace Success
>
> - Develop color-code system for files, projects, or activities
> - Use weekly chart to identify daily work activities
> - Use the services of a professional organizer
> - Use a job coach to teach/reinforce organization skills
> - Assign a mentor to help employee
> - Allow supervisor to prioritize tasks
> - Assign new project only when previous project is complete
> - Provide a "cheat sheet" of high-priority activities, projects, people, etc.
>
> (JAN 2013, pp.6–7)

WHEN TO SCREEN FOR SUBSTANCE USE

Professionals who work in the autism or medical field may be another risk factor for those with an early diagnosis of autism in that they assume autism's natural protective factors will prevail and may even be inadvertently enabling some of their patients. When collecting research for this book, we asked approximately 60 organizations that serve adolescents and adults diagnosed with autism if they routinely screen for substance use, and from those that replied, all but one said no. Many shared that SUD was simply not a priority given all the other issues an adolescent or adult with autism might encounter, such as low employment, social isolation, anxiety, depression, and struggles with daily living skills. Often people working with individuals with autism would share that substance abuse is simply too rare for them to take the time to address, even though they admitted they were unsure if their own patients might be abusing substances. To be fair, it is not only professionals who work with people with autism who don't screen for an SUD; it is all too common among mental and physical health providers (who are not working in the substance abuse field) to assume substance abuse is not an issue, and to do little more than a preliminary check without digging any deeper:

> Meanwhile, despite numerous research studies documenting high prevalence rates of substance use disorders among patients in emergency departments, hospitals, and general medical care settings, mainstream health care generally failed to recognize or address substance use disorders. In fact, a recent study by the CDC found that in 2011, only 1 in 6 United States adults and 1 in 4 binge drinkers had ever been asked by a health professional about their drinking behavior. Furthermore, the percent of adult binge drinkers who had been asked about their drinking had not changed since 1997, reflecting the challenges involved in fostering implementation of screening and counseling services for alcohol misuse in clinical settings. (US Department of Health and Human Services 2016, pp.1.19–1.20)

The combination of early interventions, a medical culture that often turns a blind eye to substance abuse, and the assumed protective factors associated with autism could lead to unfortunate overall outcomes for those on the spectrum who might be prone to addictions even if they received their diagnosis early.

Policy-wise, people in the autism community are starting to wonder if, given the reality of limited funding, so much focus on early interventions might actually be detrimental—it raises familial expectations and often doesn't appear to deliver successful long-term outcomes. Lately, more funds are being reallocated for later interventions and supports that will assist with adult independence:

> When you look at early intervention for autism, there are lots of different models, and we have a pretty good sense of evidence-based practices for young children with autism, says Leann Smith, whose research as a developmental psychologist at the University of Wisconsin at Madison focuses on adolescents and adults with autism and on their families. There isn't anything analogous to that for adults. (Carpenter 2015)

The vast majority of those with an early diagnosis and receiving treatment are still struggling with symptoms of autism. According to the *Handbook of Autism and Pervasive Developmental Disorders* (Howlin 2014), there appears to be no evidence that early childhood interventions yield better outcomes in adulthood than no ASD-specific interventions. The forecast for adult outcomes could change given the recent call for more adult studies and treatments (Howlin 2014). Currently, there is little credible literature that definitively links early interventions to a reduction in other mental health diagnoses, so it is hard to speculate whether receiving early intervention is a protective factor for someone with autism developing an SUD.

RISK FACTORS OF A LATE DIAGNOSIS

How do these risks and benefits of an early diagnosis of autism compare to being diagnosed as an adolescent or adult? As mentioned earlier, we don't really know, as there have not been many studies comparing the two. One of the obvious risks of remaining undiagnosed until late in life is the potential trauma of not fitting in, not belonging, and a feeling of constant failure:

> "Look me in the eye, young man!"
> I cannot tell you how many times I heard that shrill, whining refrain. It started about the time I got to the first grade. I heard it from parents, relatives, teachers, principals, and all manner of other people. I heard it so often I began to expect to hear it.
> Sometimes it would be punctuated by a jab from a ruler or one of those rubber tipped pointers teachers used in those days... I would glance up at their hostile faces and feel squirmier and more uncomfortable and unable to form words, and I would quickly look away. (Robinson 2007, p.1)

Numerous memoirs, essays, articles, and postings address the severe stressors undiagnosed individuals face day in and day out for feeling different than those around them. As one adult with an autism diagnosis and in recovery from alcohol addiction put it, "I didn't understand the world and the world didn't understand me" (Dave Spicer, personal interview, October 1, 2016). Anecdotally, examples used in most of the studies, books, and websites that address the intersection of ASD and SUD are individuals who lived with undiagnosed autism until adulthood. Though there are no studies to prove it, these examples give the impression that self-medication is particularly high for those diagnosed late in life:

> The resulting loneliness and social isolation individuals with ASD feel, may be exacerbated by traits such as social awkwardness and inability to convey sensitivity to others. The use of substances, such as alcohol, may initiate them into a "subculture" which does not require extensive communication, yet provides the social acceptance they seek—although potentially at the risk of exploitation and consequent alcohol dependence. (Rengit *et al.* 2016, p.2517)

Misdiagnosis seems to have had a profound impact on many individuals who sought and received less than satisfactory treatment for their symptoms:

> Matt and I felt that he could not be the only person who has managed life with undiagnosed AS by using an artificial means of controlling anxiety. In fact, it's a widely accepted means amongst the general population: "Dutch Courage" we say, when we need to combat fear by knocking back a beer or two. (Tinsley and Hendrickx 2008, p.10)

PROTECTIVE FACTORS OF A LATE DIAGNOSIS

Compared to the enormous burden of struggling through life knowing that one is different, and not being able to figure out why, the benefits of receiving a diagnosis late in life seem meager, and yet, there appear to be some positive outcomes for some, despite having weathered life without an appropriate diagnosis or treatment. One advantage is related to expectations. Usually when an individual or a group has interventions and supports in place, there is the expectation that they will improve over time, but this may not be the case once a child with an autism diagnosis becomes an adolescent:

> The fact that so many of the students interviewed for this study had a difficult time explaining the nature of their special needs and abilities (independent of whether they know their diagnosis) or underestimated the level of academic and social challenges they experience (at least as compared with parents) remains a concern. It appeared as though some students were struggling with self-acceptance or had not been provided with adequate alternatives for how to frame the nature of their exceptionality. (Camarena and Sarigiani 2009, p.126)

Those who receive a diagnosis of autism in adulthood were expected to be "normal" all their lives and they adjusted as best they could and may have developed effective coping skills to help find where they best fit rather than trying to fit in:

> As a young adult, I was lucky to discover and join the world of musicians and soundmen and special-effects people. People in those lines of work expect to deal with eccentric people. I was smart, I was capable, and I was creative, and for them that was good enough. (Robinson 2007, p.211)

Another advantage of a late diagnosis is that family members and other supports who have stood by this person do not see and treat them as a person with a diagnosis (for better or for worse); rather, they tend to see the particular individual in front of them: "One mother I spoke with said that if her son had been diagnosed when he was five years old, she might have been devastated, but his diagnosis at the age of 25 came as a relief" (Ogburn 2015). Without discounting the years of anguish and pain suffered by those who did not know they had a diagnosis, many who eventually do get diagnosed find they have a rebirth or second life, often referring to their later years as AD (after diagnosis) as opposed to BD (before diagnosis). In Jen Birch's thoughtful memoir, *Congratulations! It's Asperger's Syndrome* (2003), she breaks the book up into two sections. *Part One* is life before she had an official name for her feelings and behaviors, and *Part Two* is after she finds out she has Asperger's Syndrome. On the first page of *Part Two* she writes:

To say that this discovery was a bombshell would not be an exaggeration: it was a life-changing event. It reinterpreted most of my life in a new, understandable, and logical way. As with everything else in life, I would rather know the truth about things, the reason why something is happening in a certain way: and now, for the first time, I could understand why things had happened in certain ways. Even though I still have some of the difficulties associated with Asperger Syndrome, it helps 100 per cent to know why I am different... (Birch 2003, p.199)

The epiphany many experience becomes a new start, a new identity that can be explored and understood. For those struggling with substance abuse, it can be a profound axial shift:

This seemed much less like a diagnosis and much more like an explanation... I felt vindicated...it was real. I wasn't completely out of my mind. The ugly and fruitless cycle of "Was her head screwy and that led to drinking?" Or "Did drinking make her head screwy?" Seemed to finally be pushed aside as a pointless debate. (Regan 2014, p.12)

Another fortuitous coincidence is the rise of internet usage around the same time as the rise of adult diagnoses; this concurrence offers the chance for adolescents and adults with an autism diagnosis to connect with one another online, as Henry Kupferstein points out:

I love Facebook. It matches exactly what my needs are. I get to put out little blurbs so that people can take my "pulse" and check if I'm alive... This prevents many uncomfortable interactions that I used to avoid. I now have a tool to bypass that. (quoted in Attwood et al. 2014, p.135)

Another curveball associated with a late diagnosis is receiving it after one's child is diagnosed. Though this can be a lot at once and lead to mixed reactions, it can often lead to a unique bonding experience:

...so that finally when they suggested autism for my son, and he was evaluated and I was like "oh my god." And at that point, then all of these *whys* became *of courses*: Why did I struggle so much? Why was this or that so hard? Why did I seek to self-medicate? Why was I good at this thing but this other thing blew up? I could look at those same things and say "of course." Of course that went badly, of course I had trouble with that...and my whole life finally started making sense. (Dave Spicer, personal interview, October 1, 2016)

For this individual, his son's diagnosis clearly helped this father to understand himself better. When asked if before his diagnosis he drank to self-medicate, he agreed, but then quickly qualified that, "There are some people on the autism spectrum that don't drink because they don't want to lose control, that they are fighting to keep control already and my [adult] son is in that category...he wants nothing to do with drinking" (Dave Spicer, personal interview, October 1, 2016). This father's ability to bond with his son over the similarities of their autism and differences of their substance use seems helpful for this parent's own recovery as well as a means to explore commonalities and differences with his child.

OVERALL CHALLENGES FOR ADULTS DIAGNOSED EARLY AND LATE

What is most notable about adult outcomes for those who are on the autism spectrum is, despite when they received interventions, the outcomes are bleak. Over 85 percent of adults with an ASD in their twenties in the US are living with their parents (Poon and Sidhu 2017), "...and many individuals with ASD find themselves falling 'off a cliff' into unstructured and overwhelming adult environments for which they lack the tools for successful integration" (Wallace *et al.* 2016 pp.8–9). Although anecdotally those with a late diagnosis appear to be turning to illegal drugs or alcohol to self-medicate, the stressors of low independence, high unemployment, and uncertain community and social support seem to be the same for both those diagnosed with autism early or late in their lives. Given the current statistics for adults with autism, it's possible that anyone feeling anxious, depressed, and socially isolated might seek solace via mind-altering substances. What is important is to not have preconceived expectations. Individuals who are working in the field of general medicine or substance use should keep in mind the features of autism, and seek an evaluation if they suspect autism might be in play. And those working with individuals with an ASD should not assume protective factors such as rule-following or sensory issues might dissuade their clients from seeking relief or acceptance via alcohol or drugs. As one person with autism shared:

> I've found that, as those in AA joke about "normies," those with autism/Asperger's refer to "neurotypicals" or "NTs." Just as "normies" don't understand alcoholism or see what the big deal is with quitting, "NTs" are just as uninformed about autism. I'm finding the need to educate my sponsor and other NT friends in AA about my condition. It's interesting being in meetings now, recognizing the similarities but now also understanding the differences. (SoberRecovery Forums June 10, 2012)

CHAPTER 6

WHAT'S WRONG WITH SELF-MEDICATION?

In *Parallel Play* (2009, p.110), Tim Page lays out a striking defense for his drinking:

> I far prefer the physical act of drinking to the condition of being drunk. I've cut back dramatically on several occasions and quit once altogether, during which time I suffered no withdrawal symptoms but felt a huge surge in my social awkwardness that grew worse with each passing month. When I wasn't at work, I sat in my apartment, rocking back and forth, playing the same music over and over while watching the Weather Channel on cable television with the sound turned off. I had by then been diagnosed with Asperger's syndrome and, once I returned to wine again, it felt as though I had reintroduced a central solvent that my body chemistry had been missing for the better part of a year. I am not inclined to repeat the experiment.

This quote is unusual in that it is hard to tease out if Page is alluding to dependence, self-medication, denial, or simply typical drinking described with an unusual specificity. On first reading, we could conclude that Page is dependent on alcohol. But if alcohol is not having a negative impact on his life, is it okay that Page be dependent? If alcohol helps Page to function without anxiety, is that acceptable? Is Page self-aware enough to know if and when his reliance on alcohol has turned into dependence? Ultimately, this quote illustrates the questions that can arise when addressing self-determination.

Earlier in this book there was discussion of "self-medication." This is a popular theory among many inside and outside the field of substance abuse, but it doesn't feel quite accurate since it presupposes that an individual uses drugs or alcohol to treat a diagnosis but doesn't account for why a particular individual might choose a particular substance. Expectancy theory has been proposed as a substitute for self-medication as it addresses the expectations an individual may have regarding the use of a particular substance and how it might fulfill those beliefs. For someone with social anxiety like Page, if the expectation is that alcohol will enable social facilitation, they might drink at a gathering or party (Clarke *et al.* 2016). In a study of substance use among individuals with either an ASD or ADHD, half of the ASD participants were seeking total abstinence while the other half reported they would prefer to continue controlled substance use, since it "makes it easier for them to socially interact by helping them stay focused, regulating agitation, reducing restlessness, and allowing them to relax" (Kronenberg *et al.* 2015, p.245).

SELF-DETERMINATION IN THE AUTISM COMMUNITY

Currently the autism treatment and substance dependence professions appear to embrace different approaches. This is not to say that they don't have commonalities—they do—but for the most part, their approaches to treatment do not align. In the arena of self-determination, this can be problematic. We go into the differences and commonalities in more detail in the next chapter, but the underlying fundamental discrepancies need to be addressed when it comes to the conflict between dignity versus risk. Currently in the disabilities/autism field, after a long and complicated history of practitioners and family deciding what is in the best interests for their patients or kin, there has been a strong shift toward enabling the differently-abled person to have autonomy and self-determination. Of course, when the individual with autism is a child, making decisions in the child's best interests is a common course of action. But this approach, which in the past also included unwarranted institutionalization, was often carried out as the child aged, and might result in the infantilization and disempowerment of adults with an ASD. In recent years "self-advocacy" has been the rallying cry for adults and their supports across the spectrum. This shift has affected policy (Americans with Disabilities Act), education (Individual with Disabilities Education Act), and treatment. Deinstitutionalization was a major shift for those diagnosed with developmental delays or mental illness. Though deinstitutionalization and other policy changes that offer more opportunities for integration into society have led to autonomy and independence, it also opened up a Pandora's box of risks, including developing drug/alcohol dependence. Current approaches for those with autism, intellectual delays, and mental illness are much more appealing than the older practice of warehousing in institutions, but due to lack of resources, outcomes for adults, particularly those with autism, are still poor, which certainly puts them at risk for drug and alcohol use (Burgard *et al.* 2000; Chowdhury and Benson 2011). Most of the literature regarding the impact of drug and alcohol abuse addresses those with intellectual delays. There are few published studies regarding those with an ASD and SUD, and they have different findings. A 2017 comprehensive study from Sweden has shown that individuals with an autism diagnosis have higher rates of substance use than the general population. There is no single reason for this outcome, and the authors offer several theories (Butwicka *et al.* 2017). As mentioned earlier in this book, researchers suggest a variety of explanations including genetic commonalities, behavioral similarities (repetitive behaviors), and environmental factors (including parental drug use that may cause autistic-like behaviors in their offspring) (Butwicka, *et al.* 2017). As we have stressed throughout this book, research addressing outcomes of various interventions and treatment modalities for adults on the autism spectrum, though improving, is sparse.

SELF-DETERMINATION IN THE SUD COMMUNITY

In the substance abuse field, honoring autonomy is a trickier proposition. As the writer Edward St. Aubyn's drug-abusing narrator put it, "How could he think his way out of the problem when the problem was the way he thought" (2012, p.167). When it comes to self-determination, addiction treatment is a mixed bag. Most recently, addiction treatment has moved away from the goal of recovery, instead, taking a page from the disabilities playbook and working toward maintenance. Yet the addictions field still appears to revolve around the Twelve Steps as the best approach, despite many questions regarding its efficacy (Ferri, Amato, and Davoli 2006). The overarching goal when treating someone with an SUD is abstinence. As in other medical realms this all-or-nothing way of thinking has been changing. In the medical and disability literature attitudes and vocabularies are slowly shifting; now we find semantic alterations such as *living with* rather than *curing*, or *managing* rather than *eradicating*. But there is still cognitive dissonance when it comes to expressing a more fluid outlook when treating addictions, since moderation and addiction do not appear to easily coexist. If indeed the choice is abstinence or dependence, then one's self-determination is not only called into question, but from an Alcoholics Anonymous perspective, it is actually harmful, as noted from the first of the Twelve Steps: "We admitted we were powerless over alcohol—that our lives had become unmanageable" (AA 1952).

HARM REDUCTION

The harm reduction movement is trying to change the black-and-white thinking that has dominated the SUD field for the past 50 years:

> Harm reduction incorporates a spectrum of strategies from safer use, to managed use to abstinence to meet drug users "where they're at," addressing conditions of use along with the use itself. Because harm reduction demands that interventions and policies designed to serve drug users reflect specific individual and community needs, there is no universal definition of or formula for implementing harm reduction. (Harm Reduction Coalition 2017)

Anyone connected to disability rights and services might find the language of harm reduction to be familiar, but to individuals in the field of substance abuse—except for those who are comfortable with treating opioid dependence with methadone or buprenorphine (Suboxone)—it can seem radical. And opioid replacement treatments such as methadone and buprenorphine are fraught and stigmatized. "Methadone patients are perceived as zombies and even called 'methadonians' which further alienates them from the human race. This negative image of methadone patients is opposite the facts and reality" (Woods and Joseph 2015, p.238). Replacement treatments are often looked down on and seen as "using" rather than treatment.

This leads us to examine the "dignity of risk" when it comes to substance dependence among those with an autism diagnosis. In the previous chapter we noted that anecdotally, more people diagnosed late in life were presented in studies and books that addressed the connection of autism and drug or alcohol addiction.

The go-to conclusion is: older undiagnosed individuals use substances to "self-medicate" their unnamed condition. But is it possible that those who received a diagnosis late in life were already autonomous and therefore had the fundamental right to self-determination? Self-determination may be less prevalent among adults who grew up with a diagnosis (Slayter 2007). For the most part, those having an ASD as children have had family, professionals, and the community calling the shots for them from an early age, and this may protect them from SUDs. One parent's response to the question of why his adult child with autism did not use substances illustrates this point: "Living with his parents the decision was made for him. He has never been in a situation where he had to make that decision" (Anonymous, family member survey December 5, 2016).

This is a tough balancing act. How can one help those who appear not to be able to help themselves without being paternalistic (Slayter 2007)? Slayter, in her article addressing substance abuse and treatment for those who have an intellectually challenged diagnosis (ICD), goes on to cite Deborah Stone (1997), who, in *Policy Paradox: The Art of Political Decision Making*, addresses the balance between liberty, equality, and security. Slayter (2007) recommends trying to find the best blend on a case-by-case basis in order to assure that an individual isn't forced to sacrifice liberty for the sake of security, or to sacrifice equality for the sake of liberty. What further complicates this approach is that once an individual is receiving, say, disability benefits, the government will add restrictions that could compromise a person's liberty, and so self-determination may no longer be in play (Slayter 2007).

As mentioned earlier, some individuals with autism have co-occurring intellectual challenges and some do not. Much of what Slayter addresses could easily apply to anyone with a developmental delay including autism. But autism, with or without a co-occurring ICD, can have a particular component that cannot be generalized: lack of social connectedness. Several studies of substance use among individuals with autism without a co-occurring ICD addressed two types of individuals with autism: those who want to socialize and those who do not. Though both groups may have impaired social communication due to autism, the impairment does not necessarily determine an individual's desire to socialize. As Clarke *et al.* (2016, p.156) note:

...studies have assumed that participants' diagnosis of Asperger syndrome, SUD and their interaction are solely located "within" the individual. As a result, these studies do not acknowledge, nor explore the impact of interpersonal, social, cultural and societal influences on how participants' make sense of their substance use in relation to their diagnosis.

The differences are illustrated by one adult on the spectrum who drank in order to facilitate socializing versus another individual who used substances to escape from socializing: "I have decided that I won't be quitting drinking fully because I noticed a great part of my social life will be gone and to me that's not worth it, and I don't know how it could be done without the booze" (Kronenberg *et al.* 2014, p.5); "Carl spoke of how at times he used...tobacco...as an escape from social settings: 'I start smoking. Smoking is an excuse to get out of it all. So I wind up outside with a cigarette in my mouth'" (Clarke *et al.* 2016, p.159).

EXPANDING ON SELF-MEDICATION

Earlier in this book we explored self-medication and raised questions as to whether it is always the wrong choice. Self-medication in the autism world is particularly controversial. Often children are accused of self-medicating simply by enacting certain behaviors or craving certain foods. One parent shared: "...his addiction is to sugar, and there has been speculation about the similar addictive qualities of alcohol and sugar" (Anonymous, family member survey, December 5, 2016). There are many theories and ASD treatments that target the "addictive" behaviors of children with an ASD. In the autism literature, children with a diagnosis are often suspected of self-medicating; not with alcohol or drugs, but instead, with gluten and/or casein. Books fill the autism section of bookstores addressing *leaky gut* and food allergies and other possible links between certain foods exacerbating or even causing autism. These books address the addictive nature of certain foods and revolve around the theory that these foods create a cycle of addiction: for example, ingredients in cheese and bread might increase autistic behaviors, and then these increased symptoms of autism trigger the child's brain to crave the very foods that might harm them most (Kuzemchak 2012). There are a number of parents and some professionals who refer to this cycle of impairment as leaky gut, a condition related to the gut–brain connection. The differences between leaky gut and gut–brain are important: leaky gut refers to particular food allergies, whereas gut–brain targets the bacteria and digestive complications that often accompany autism (Autism Speaks 2017b).

Many people directly connect leaky gut/gluten and casein allergies to addiction. One parent's website explains this theory:

> Our kids with autism—and hyperactivity—are extremely vulnerable to environmental toxins, and the toxins of its metabolism. There are certain elements in diet, specifically gluten and casein (dairy) that are not completely digested by many children with autism and hyperactivity. Due to insufficient digestion, gluten and casein eventually produce endogenous opioids, components of brain activity similar to morphine. Thus, the diet can have a profound effect on the brain of these children. In other words, it is as if they were "high."
>
> I know it is shocking to many, but it's true. Homeopathic doctors and nutritionists report that some autistic children when they arrive at their offices, have a vacant stare, dilated pupils, do not interact and exhibit inappropriate behavior. Moreover they seem to have an incredible craving for foods containing gluten and diary, such as chicken nugget, macaroni and cheese, ice cream, etc. (de Kwant 2016)

The purpose of this book is not to dispel or support such theories (though for those who trust the medical community, there is no empirical evidence that leaky gut is the cause of autism), but what is of interest is the perception that a child with autism could be grappling with addictions as soon as they begin to ingest solid foods. The celebrity Jenny McCarthy, who has a child diagnosed with autism, has championed diets that target leaky gut:

> I explained to Oprah that with the proper diet, kids were getting better. I talked about the gut–brain connection... A doctor once said to me that if people don't believe in the gut–brain connection, then tell them to go try that theory in a bar. Order a drink and see what happens. (McCarthy 2008, p.10)

The doctor is right, something does happen, but what happens is complex and nuanced. Some might say it depends on the drink, or how much is consumed; others might say it depends on who's drinking;

and still others might conclude it is a combination of a variety of environmental and biological factors. Ultimately, McCarthy's doctor's analogy to alcohol's impact is not so simple. Most individuals working in the field of substance abuse would say that it really depends on a *particular* individual's gut and brain.

The way the brain works in substance abuse is complicated. Most treatment modalities target triggers and cravings. Different substances can impact different parts of the brain and long-term use then affects other parts of the brain. A trigger—defined as stimuli that lead to a desire (craving) to use an addictive substance—often results in substance use that can lead to a cycle of substance abuse. For children with ASD there are cravings for particular reasons that may not only lead to self-harm, as many of those who advocate against casein and gluten sometimes suggest (McCarthy and Kartzinel 2010). It is important to consider that it may not always be the food's nutritional properties that account for certain cravings among children with an autism diagnosis. Occupational therapists and dieticians have found, given the sensory issues for those on the spectrum, that intense desire for a certain texture over another is a common occurrence for children with an ASD (Cermak, Curtin, and Bandini 2010). Many children with an autism diagnosis have frustratingly limited diets—one mother told me that for several months her toddler would only eat fish sticks: "fish-sticks for breakfast, lunch and dinner" (Anonymous communication, September 12, 2016). Her pediatrician considered this a sensory issue, and recommended the mother just wait it out, continue to serve the child what the rest of the family was eating, occasionally introduce new foods, and eventually the child would change on his own. But when the mother mentioned her son's extreme dietary limitations to an occupational therapist, the therapist agreed it was a sensory issue, and told the mother that she had to break this habit immediately or the child would always have problems. These two different recommendations by professionals are reminiscent of the theories of harm reduction versus abstinence.

PARENTS' TREATMENT CHOICES

There are well over 100 documented treatments for autism, though few have been studied thoroughly enough to prove their efficacy (Goin-Kochel, Myers, and Mackintosh 2007; Green *et al.* 2006).

Along with treatments such as chelation (a detoxification treatment), aromatherapy and Interactive Metronome (a physiological treatment) are pharmacological options that include Ativan, Xanax, Clonopin, Ritilan, and Adderall (all of which have the potential for being abused) (Goin-Kochel *et al.* 2007; Green *et al.* 2006). We can add MDMA (Ecstasy) and marijuana treatments to the list, given their recent popularity. When it comes to treatment, the famous adage seems to apply: "If you've met one person with autism, you've met one person with autism." Unlike some therapies such as aromatherapy or baby massage, which appear to be relatively benign, other interventions (often endorsed by parents) might seem risky or even dangerous. In the autism community, it is not unusual to read or hear comments from parents accusing other parents of child abuse, for either recommending or avoiding particular interventions:

> I came home one day a few months after my child had been diagnosed and in my mailbox was an article about how a certain diet would cure my child's autism. No note or name on it. Not many people knew about the diagnosis yet. Not many people had a clue of all the treatments (speech and occupational therapy, social skills, a special preschool etc.) we were already trying. My son was very underweight and a picky eater. The diet in that article seemed impossible to implement. I believe whoever left it meant to help but it made me feel helpless, horrible and angry. (Anonymous communication, December 11, 2016)

Why address parents' treatment choices for their children with an ASD? There appears to be a parallel to individuals with an ASD making choices for themselves. In both cases, treatment choices are nuanced and complicated, and the burden on parents to determine what is best for their child appears particularly fraught. To some of us, a parent not implementing a recommended diet that could improve the child's outcome may be viewed as a crime; to others, implementing it and not letting the child enjoy foods he likes, especially if he's underweight, could seem equally criminal. Balancing the risks and outcomes are particularly tricky.

The ethics of making choices on behalf of children, the differently-abled, the intoxicated, or impaired are messy and complicated. When an adult with autism states:

so why not use marihuana in the same way? i can confirm that in my case, it helps calm me down after overload, it has prevented complete meltdowns, it's more efficient than alcohol in letting me cope with social situations such as parties (especially with loud music) because i'm not as proned to make a fool of myself seeing as my awareness is higher on marihuana than alcohol. sometimes it also helps me to stop my brain from rambling when i'm trying to get to sleep. although i'm fairly sure there are many alternatives out there (Rachel's weighted blanket as an example probably does pretty much the same job for her as a small joint for me) when it comes down to it, i think people should do whatever works for them, as long as nobody – including themselves – gets harmed in the process. (Anonymous communication, November 29, 2009)

Who is to say this adult is wrong? And though this individual's declaration may seem reasonable and rational, it may read differently when juxtaposed to the worries of the parents of a teen with autism whose marijuana use appears less benign: "The scary thing is that I fear that marijuana has become his new 'obsession.' He admitted to daily use and has told me on more than one occasion that he has no intentions of stopping. He sees it as a harmless, 'natural' substance" (Hutten 2010). Putting aside the fact that marijuana is not harmless where it is illegal and can do great harm if a teen is arrested, how can we judge what therapy may be working? Do we find alternatives? And what alternatives are viable? As one parent of a child with autism suggested, the drugs they have been prescribed sometimes seem more dangerous than alcohol or marijuana:

Having spent half the night looking into this subject I see now that scientists are coming to the realization that marijuana might be useful in treating autism. My son was taking zoloft. We looked it up after our doctor told us there are no studies on how these drugs affect kids. They do know it causes cellular changes in the young brain, but do not know what harm these changes can cause over time. Nice huh... Yeah let's stick with what's legal. What a joke. (Smith 2011)

This father has a point since recent studies suggest that though there may be some benefit of prescribing SSRIs (selective serotonin reuptake inhibitors) such as Zoloft, there are not enough robust studies to prove the benefits of SSRIs outweigh the negative impact (Kolevzon, Mathewson, and Hollander 2006; McPheeters *et al.* 2011).

ALCOHOL AND RECREATIONAL DRUGS AS TREATMENT FOR AUTISM

There is no easy answer to the questions raised addressing a parent's choices or a self-advocate's self-determination in relation to using illegal drugs or alcohol to informally "treat" the symptoms of autism. Searching the internet yields an array of iffy treatments that may or not be beneficial. There are apparently legitimate clinical trials now underway researching the impact of MDMA (known as Ecstasy or Molly on the street):

> There are currently no FDA-approved pharmacological treat-ments for autistic adults with social anxiety, and conventional anti-anxiety medications lack clinical effectiveness in this population. Based on anecdotal reports, MDMA-assisted therapy may be a suitable intervention for the treatment of social anxiety in autistic adults and warrants further investigation in a randomized controlled clinical trial. (MAPS 2015)

A search of the internet finds a wealth of sites and postings dedicated to cannabis as an effective treatment for autism, despite few, if any, clinical trials:

> With regard to human data on use of cannabis for developmental and behavioral conditions, to our knowledge, the only available data are from small case series [small descriptive studies that track patients] or single studies... In sum, none of these studies provide sufficient, high-quality data to suggest that cannabis should be recommended for treatment of ASD or ADHD at this time...
> ...Even if and when studies on cannabis for developmental and behavioral conditions are conducted, they will likely use formulations of oral dronabinol or cannabidiol, both of which can be administered with a known dose and predictable schedule; at this time, the bulk of medical marijuana is sold in plant form, which results in a highly variable dose of active compound and with less predictable onset of effect based on whether it is inhaled or ingested. (Hadland, Knight, and Harris 2015, p.8)

For self-advocates and family members, it is hard to know which treatments are healthy and which are harmful. For some with autism, psychedelics may seem like an ideal treatment:

> I also have the super-fun Aspergers/ADHD/Depression/Anxiety cocktail. Magic mushrooms have given me the ability to help me identify certain problems in my life and then take the steps towards fixing them. They have also pulled me out of suicidal depression more than once, quite literally saving my life. I also find that when I am tripping, or right after, I can understand people's emotions in a way that I normally can't access—almost like the veil of autism is being peeled away for a few hours. (Shroomery.org January 24, 2017)

But others may take the same drug and find it extremely detrimental and even dangerous:

> Aspies often get overwhelmed by too much stimulation and Mushrooms was WAAAAAAYYYYYY too much stimulation for me to handle. On a bad trip, I couldn't look anyone in the face. I couldn't put sentences [sic] together. I would see screaming faces coming at me that werent' [sic] there. Strange (seemingly random) patterns appreared [sic] to be engraved on every surface (even my skin!). Some trips hit me so hard that I would collapse (even though I was on a VERY low dose). I didn't want to be around anyone, and if I was around anyone, they had to speak slowly and softly to me otherwise I felt very afraid. I do not recommend mushrooms for Aspies unless you intend to tackle your darkest inner demons. (Shroomery.org April 10, 2014)

How does a loved one or professional value the person's autonomy and at the same time, keep them safe? Searching autism forums such as Wrong Planet and Reddit, there is a great deal of discussion among individuals on the autism spectrum regarding (mostly the benefits of) alcohol, benzodiazepines (Xanax, Valium, Ativan, Klonopin), cannabis (marijuana, hashish), MDMA (Ecstasy), and LSD and other hallucinogens and opioids. As mentioned earlier, some individuals with autism say these substances have significantly improved functioning, while others share that these drugs caused debilitating dysfunction; and then there are those who find drugs or alcohol have had little impact one way or the other.

People with autism are said to have concrete thinking: literal, functional, and often black or white. They are also said to be rule-followers. Most children are taught that alcohol/drugs are addictive and so alcohol and drugs are bad. Many trust in that rule. But as we know, the rules change as a child ages. As Glenna Osborne, Director of Transition to Adult Services at the University of North Carolina (UNC) TEACCH Autism Program shared about "B," an adult client with ASD who struggled with alcohol addiction:

> There was a lot of loneliness and boredom. Not knowing what to do with his time. He had a lot of misconceptions of what other people do. He asked "doesn't everybody my age go out on Friday and Saturday nights and get drunk?" Osborne elaborated that B had made his assumptions from movies, TV and social media. When I said "no" not everyone gets drunk on the weekends he was shocked. (Glenna Osborne, personal interview, March 7, 2017)

For neurotypical as well as neuroatypical children, the antisubstance use rules change as they age and begin to put more trust in their peers' rules. This is particularly true for someone who may feel like an outsider among their peers. Mike Chapman, Director of Supported Employment at the UNC TEACCH Autism Program, noted:

> If they fit in they [teens with autism] tend to fit in with the alternative crowd, tended to be the ones more likely to have recreational drug use...later there's more depression. They remember "what did I use to do when I had fun?" and they fall back onto drugs. (Mike Chapman, personal interview, January 17, 2017)

Another assumption about individuals with an ASD is that they will be direct and literal about their substance use, but as one therapist explained, the concrete thinking of a person with an ASD can result in distorted perceptions of their actions: "if they [adults with an ASD] drink and don't resemble how addiction is portrayed in movies or on TV they don't see what they're doing as a problem" (Glenna Osborne, personal interview, March 7, 2017). Or, as a young man with an autism diagnosis explained to his mother, who warned him repeatedly about addiction running in the family: "He said he didn't have a problem with alcohol because he had been drinking with a friend off and on for about a month and was not addicted. I had to explain that addiction doesn't usually happen in a month" (Glenna

Osborne, personal interview, March 7, 2017). The misconception that dependence happens immediately and is not a slow process can lead to dangerous consequences. Substance dependence is a learned behavior with negative outco. The challenge of navigating drug/alcohol use in everyday life is a balancing act for loved ones and for professionals. What parent wouldn't want their child with autism to enjoy the neurotypical ritual of a drink with a friend? One parent of an adult with autism wrote, "Wouldn't mind him trying a beer to see if he likes it but he won't try it" (Anonymous, parent survey, November 22, 2016). Like many parents, this person may enjoy the "normalness" of his adult son having a beer with a friend, but most likely would balk if the friendship depended on drinking beer.

Though professionals and family members are expected to honor self-determination, along with acceptance they must also provide guidance, and not placidly allow self-harming behaviors if they are truly detrimental. Of course it is hard to make the call on behalf of another person, but it may be worse not to intervene. What is striking is how few bother to investigate if addictive substances may already be in play: "…for years, the assumption remained that addiction was one concern the autism community could safely ignore" (Szalavitz 2017).

Given recent studies implicating that individuals with autism may be at a higher risk for substance dependence than the general population (Butwicka et al. 2017), and the steady increase of adults diagnosed with ASD (CDC 2016), it is imperative that education, screenings, and treatment become refined and routine.

CHAPTER 7

SCREENING, TREATMENT, AND PREVENTION

As noted earlier, the famous adage among the autism community, "if you've met one person with autism, you've met one person with autism," can easily translate to the field of substance use diagnoses (Szalavitz 2016). A broad swath of the population is affected by both diagnoses, and each individual can present very differently. Some adults with autism have dual or even multi-diagnoses, and so treatment should be tailored to address their particular presentations (Autism Society 2016). In the field of SUD, not only do patients have comorbidities, but distinctive substance use problems need to be treated differently; someone dependent on cocaine may need a particular treatment protocol that might be significantly different than someone being treated for alcohol use disorder (SAMHSA 2016b). A major difference regarding the treatment approaches of these two diagnoses is that, until recently, most SUD interventions have followed a mental health model of treatment with a focus on medications, counseling, and peer support, whereas autism treatment, because autism is considered a global developmental delay, has an overarching approach that focuses on psycho-educational treatment including social skills training, attention to daily living skills, educational, and vocational support (NIDA 2016; NIH 2017b). Of course, treatments for both diagnoses have some overlap, and providers, particularly in the field of SUD, are beginning to explore the effectiveness of offering global treatment options to their patients, broadening the focus from behavioral interventions, and adding community reinforcement strategies such as vouchers, housing assistance, and vocational counseling (SAMHSA 2017a). The different treatment modalities and approaches for each diagnosis is the topic for several books; for the purposes of this book, the focus of this chapter is on screening, assessment, and how to capitalize on existing treatments by tailoring them to an individual with a dual ASD and SUD diagnosis.

Now that studies regarding the long-term outcomes of adults with autism are starting to trickle in, there are several interesting findings, with some surprising overlaps. For instance, studies show those with an autism diagnosis have higher rates of gender variance than the general population. As a result, professionals who work with patients questioning their gender identity are encouraged to screen for autism (Strang *et al.* 2016). As mentioned throughout this book, recent studies show higher rates of substance use among those with autism. If people presenting with gender identity issues should be screened for ASD, we could also suggest that individuals with an SUD also be screened for an ASD. But given the higher numbers of those presenting with substance abuse concerns (8.4 percent of the adult population in the US) than gender identity concerns (a rough estimate of 0.3 percent of the US adult population), the hurdles of implementing such a screening could be prohibitive (Butwicka *et al.* 2017; Gates 2011). Knowing that the rate of substance use is higher within the transgender community could put those in that community with an autism diagnosis at even higher risk (US Department of Health and Human Services 2016). These various overlaps of presentations and diagnoses call for heightened awareness of what to be looking for when an individual is seeking treatment. Providers need to stay abreast of current statistics as well as pay attention to the commonalities and differences of who is walking through their door.

As mentioned earlier in this book, there are several mental health diagnoses that can accompany an ASD. Along with those often-documented such as anxiety, depression, OCD, and ADHD, there are reports of increased suicidal and self-harming behaviors (Hannon and Taylor 2013; Maddox, Trubanova, and White 2016). The once-assumed protective factors of an autism diagnosis do not seem to have an impact when it comes to self-harming behaviors, and there have been calls for more research to understand the root of these worrying comorbidities. It is critical that those who work in mental health settings be prepared to advance cross-system collaborations in order to provide targeted and comprehensive treatment options (Slayter and Steenrod 2009).

WHY SCREEN FOR SUBSTANCE USE?

Now that autism is no longer seen as a protective factor for developing an addiction, it is essential to address how to reduce this comorbidity between ASD and SUD via proper screenings, environmental support, targeted treatments, and accurate educational outreach. Though it may not be viable for professionals in the substance abuse field to learn to screen for autism, the more practical approach would be for those who work with teenagers and adults with autism to routinely screen for substance abuse. Screening for suicide among those with an ASD is already beginning to be implemented. When we first started researching this book we consulted a forum of distinguished autism professionals. When the topic of substance use among the ASD population was raised, it was promptly dropped, and the discussion shifted to recently implemented screening protocols for suicidality. Though screening for suicidality is critical, no connection was made to screening for SUD, a risk factor for suicide (CDC 1999).

The autism community should not be singled out for under-screening substance use. Most addiction professionals would agree that the medical community does not screen enough for SUD. As the office of the Surgeon General's report on addiction in America (2016, pp.19–20) emphasizes:

> ...despite numerous research studies documenting high prevalence rates of substance use disorders among patients in emergency departments, hospitals, and general medical care settings, mainstream health care generally failed to recognize or address substance use disorders. In fact, a recent study by the CDC [Centers for Disease Control] found that in 2011, only 1 in 6 United States adults and 1 in 4 binge drinkers had *ever* been asked by a health professional about their drinking behavior... This has been a costly mistake, with often deadly consequences. A recent study showed that the presence of a substance use disorder often doubles the odds for the subsequent development of chronic and expensive medical illnesses, such as arthritis, chronic pain, heart disease, stroke, hypertension, diabetes, and asthma.

Surprisingly, alcohol and drug screenings have only recently been introduced in hospital emergency departments.

Emergency departments are logical places to use the questionnaire (drug and alcohol) because they often see the direct or indirect impact of substance use or abuse. Up to 40 percent of all hospital beds in the US—except for those being used by maternity and intensive care patients—are being used to treat health conditions related to alcohol consumption, according to the National Council on Alcoholism and Drug Dependence.

Alcoholism is the third leading lifestyle-related cause of death and tobacco is the first, according to the Centers for Disease Control and Prevention (CDC) (Ochs 2016). In the US, opioid overdose is the leading cause of death for adults under 50.

Given the high rates of substance abuse, it is startling how few primary care settings screen for it, but screening is increasing in the US due, in part, to the Affordable Care Act (ACA). The ACA mandated insurance companies offer payment parity for mental health and substance abuse treatment. This helped to remove the stigma, and allowed for these conditions to be treated no differently than physical health conditions. Parity also allowed healthcare professionals to offer a broader systematic level of care—with some primary care settings going so far as to integrate social workers and counselors into their practice—and offering substance abuse and mental health treatment options to patients who were previously lacking due to insurers not covering mental health/substance abuse treatments (Padwa *et al.* 2012; White 2014). Although there is no solid evidence that screenings are always effective, addressing issues like domestic violence, mental health, and other seemingly unrelated yet intrinsically connected factors that contribute to an individual's health outcomes, and then offering appropriate (and if possible, on-site) services could be incorporated into physical healthcare settings (Hoge *et al.* 2014). Yet, addressing substance use and dependence in primary care settings is still not a priority. For some patients, not screening for potential SUDs could be a matter of life and death, as one individual with an opioid addiction shared: "I had over five years clean. I had to have emergency surgery and told the people who admitted me to the hospital not to use opioids. Clearly that information never got passed on and the minute I felt the Fentanyl go in me, I knew my sobriety was over" (Anonymous communication, October 9, 2016).

Screening for substance abuse for those working with adolescents and adults with autism should be the norm, but from the literature posted and responses received when researching this book, it appears screenings are infrequent. "A recent review found that screening for

SUD among individuals with ASD is not part of routine clinical assessments in psychiatry, although SUD screening is increasingly an integral part of clinical guidelines for many other conditions" (Arnevik and Helverschou 2016, p.69).

For this book, we sent out surveys to a broad range of professionals working with adolescents and adults with an ASD. They were asked to share their experiences working with someone with an autism diagnosis who was grappling with an SUD. The majority of people contacted reported their experience of an SUD/ASD dual diagnosis was *not common, seldom* or *never*. One organization shared: "We are now thinking of asking [about substance use] during our intake for the…coaching program where we work more intensely one-on-one with folks. After working with someone for a while we usually can tell but it's also possible that it is hidden" (Dania Jekel, personal communication, January 12, 2017). A minority of the professionals contacted did reply that they have encountered SUD among the individuals they worked with: "It is not uncommon for me either in my role as the director of a support program for college students with ASD, or in my private practice, to deal with substance use. I would guess that it occurs in 10–15% of the individuals that I work with" (Mitchell Nagler, personal communication, February 22, 2017).

As of 2013, the statistics for abuse and dependence among young adults in the general population was 13 percent for alcohol and 7.4 percent for illegal drugs, so, according to Mitchell Nagler's personal experience, college students with an official diagnosis of autism appear to have no more protective factors and possibly greater risk factors than the general population (SAMHSA 2014).

Another professional who works with supported employment noted that drug and alcohol use was a common occurrence among her clientele with autism. Like the rest of the providers we had contacted, initially this provider thought the protective factors of autism— rule-following, social impairment, and sensory issues—would make substance abuse a rare occurrence among her clients, and never screened for substance abuse:

> We learn from our mistakes, right? We would be trying to get a job for someone and the job required a drug screening and drugs were not on our radar so we said to the employer "no problem" and then they [clients with autism] would fail the screening. Once that

started happening, we started screening all our clients. (Glenna Osborne, personal interview, March 7, 2017)

From the anecdotal evidence collected for this book, it would appear that those who screen for SUD among their clients with autism diagnosis find higher rates of SUD. Most likely the same could be said the other way round, that if professionals in the field of substance abuse screened for autism, they might find higher rates of ASD among their patients than they may have suspected.

IS IT AUTISM? FOR ADDICTION SPECIALISTS, FAMILY MEMBERS, AND SELF-ADVOCATES

The key to screening for substance abuse is asking. As one supported employment counselor reported:

> I had a client that I was providing job coaching services to and became aware that he was abusing alcohol, by asking him. I believe that he was aware it was not normal to consume the amount of alcohol he was consuming or at the times of day he was consuming the alcohol, but did not know how to seek help or how to stop on his own and was embarrassed by his behavior. (Jayson Delisle, professionals survey, February 9, 2017)

To understand the seriousness and range of use there are particular screenings for different types of substances. For those working with individuals with ASD, employing basic screenings for substance use and offering follow-up treatment may be a start to an intervention. The same is not true for professionals who work in substance abuse and addictions. As with any patient, neurotypical or neuroatypical, the individual needs to be sober when being assessed. Withdrawal from the substance of choice may present a host of issues including anxiety, depression, and sometimes even hallucinations, making it hard to sort out whether autism is in the mix. And prior diagnoses can persist even if there are indications that they may not be accurate. It is important that if clinicians suspect a different or additional diagnosis than the one attached to a client on intake, they advocate for the client, and try to get a more accurate assessment (Lewis 2016). Providing a thorough assessment may not be easy to do with limited funding, but would be worth the effort if the resulting diagnosis matched the patient with appropriate services, offered proper treatment options, and possibly brought peace of mind. Autism does not present in a clear-cut manner, especially in adults, and appearances can be deceiving:

> I'm often told that you wouldn't know I have Asperger's to look at me. I've had a quarter of a century to craft my front, and the art of "pretending to be normal" is something that I have finely tuned over the years. However, even though I look pretty normal (at least in a Hell's Angels kind of way), the quirks start to show when you dig a little deeper. My hair is long because I can't stand having my hair cut... The jeans and t-shirt seem innocuous enough, but only once I've actually bought them. Navigating rows of t-shirts, feeling through till I get the right one... As for jeans...finding ones that fit exactly, that are made of the right material, not too scratchy, not too soft... I dye my hair to stand out, fine. However, the reason behind this is that if I look a little different, I find it a lot easier to come across as eccentric when I make the inevitable social faux pas that go hand in hand with Asperger's... While we have diagnostic criteria for the diagnosis of Asperger's Syndrome and autism spectrum disorders, the traits vary wildly from person to person... For example, people with AS are known to have problems with eye contact... I maintain pretty decent eye contact when I first meet someone, which tends to become more hit and miss as I get to know them, in that I feel more comfortable being myself. (Jackson 2016, pp.22–23)

One sign family members, friends, and clinicians should be on the lookout for is intense and unabated anxiety after withdrawal. There are two identified phases of withdrawal:

- Acute withdrawal occurs during the detoxification process and can last a couple of days to a couple of weeks depending on the drug.

- Protracted withdrawal can persist for a much longer period of time and can impact sleep, concentration, depression, irritability and, of course, anxiety.

(SAMHSA 2010)

It is important for everyone involved to know that protracted withdrawal can sometimes last over a year. Although anxiety during acute and protracted withdrawal is common, if the anxiety persists months past detoxification, it may be a sign of *symptom rebound*, that is, the return of the anxiety, depression, insomnia, etc. that may have instigated the substance use in the first place. These symptoms do not resolve since, as noted earlier in this book, they often prompt the *self-medication*. Research indicates that those with ASD who have developed an addiction often do so to stave off intense anxiety (Tinsley and Hendrickx 2008). Withdrawing from their substance of choice could present an extreme level of anxiety.

POSSIBLE SIGNS OF A DUAL SUBSTANCE USE/AUTISM DIAGNOSIS

Other possible signs a patient with an SUD who might also have an ASD are as follows:

- Poor eye contact. As Luke Jackson (2016) observed, if there is eye contact, be aware of the character of an individual's eye contact: it may be limited, too intense, or not seem direct (looking at you, but not into your eyes).

- Mannered or overly formal way of speaking, a literalness, bluntness, or directness that may seem abrupt or even rude (depending on what your cultural background is).

- A stiff or vaguely awkward gait and other slightly unusual physical mannerisms.

- Heightened sensitivities to light, tastes, textures, sounds, or smells.

- Insistence on sticking to routines.

- Unusually intense or focused interests.

If a clinician unfamiliar with autism suspects an ASD, it is recommended they read about autism and the various ways it can present (The Autism Society and Autism Speaks websites in the US and The National Autistic Society website in the UK are good places to start).

If appropriate, it might be worth asking some questions about the patient's social life, habits, interests, and childhood to get a better picture:

- "Do you have close friends?" "Did you have close friends in childhood?" "Did/do you have difficulty making friends?"

- "What were your interests when you were a child?" "Did you have any particular or special interests you pursued?" Even if the interests may seem routine, like Heavy Metal music, it may be worth digging deeper to find out just how involved the patient was. As noted earlier in this book, if the interest involves detailed specifics including every venue a band may have played in, or knowing a band's exact tour dates from 2002, that might be a red flag.

- Some targeted questions regarding sensory issues might be warranted; for instance, if they drink, "Do you like drinking in bars or clubs?" and if the answer is no, a follow-up of "What don't you like about bars or clubs?" If the reasons are mostly sensory—the smell, the noise, the crowds, etc.—this might be helpful. Conversely, do not dismiss an answer of yes, since sensory issues may also apply (depending on the bar), such as dark, quiet, and calm.

Of course, if autism is suspected, be careful how the diagnosis is raised. Although much of the writing by those diagnosed in adulthood state they felt intense relief upon receiving an accurate diagnosis, it is important to remember that the patient is, in that moment, grappling with trying to cope without their substance of choice.

People with Asperger's drink for a very good reason: it is in some cases the only way they know how to exist in the world. Removing the protective layer against the confusions and expectations of a social world may unearth high levels of anxiety and depression.

> Managing anxiety must go hand-in-hand with the withdrawal of alcohol as the AS perspective of the AS alcoholic may be different to the neurotypical alcoholic. An AS alcoholic needs to learn how to cope with the world whilst being under the hold of alcohol, as the desire to return to using alcohol will be very strong. (Johnson 2017)

It is important to ensure that the individual is stable and can manage the prospect of a new diagnosis since ultimately, the proper diagnosis can bring targeted treatment and hopefully, relief. If a clinician or loved one suspects autism and the individual displaying the traits is not interested or rejects pursuing the diagnosis, try to weigh the balance of self-determination and harm reduction.

> I had a young male patient grappling with opioid addiction who I suspected had autism. I considered pursuing this diagnosis. I noticed he had disability insurance, and I asked him how he qualified. He didn't answer. I wondered if he already had an autism diagnosis and didn't want to self-identify. I decided to back off for the time being and just address the addiction. (Elizabeth Kunreuther, March 23, 2017)

When screening for autism, it is recommended that there be a thorough assessment—especially for adolescents and adults—since there are many other diagnoses such as social anxiety disorder, avoidant personality disorder, OCD/ADHD, schizophrenia (and other thought disorders), or narcissistic disorder, that may look like ASD but may require a very different treatment regiment. Screening procedures vary, and there is a lot to keep in mind:

- There are some preliminary screening tools such as the Ritvo Autism Asperger Diagnostic Scale (RAADS) 14 Screen found online (and the abridged version, RAADS-R) (Ritvo *et al.* 2008) that could be helpful for those working in SUD settings to see if their patients might need a thorough assessment for autism (Eriksson, Andersen, and Bejerot 2016).

- Many mental health assistance organizations in the US, such as a state's vocational rehabilitation or disability program, may require certain tests be administered. It is critical for clinicians to check with local agencies to see if they require particular assessments before moving forward. For example, in order for some states to offer ASD targeted interventions for a newly diagnosed patient, Adaptive Behavioral Scales such as the Vineland or Adaptive Behavior Assessment System (ABAS) must be completed.

- The "gold standard" for diagnostic evaluation appears to be one done by a multidisciplinary team that includes the Autism Diagnostic Interview-Revised (ADI-R) and Autism Diagnostic Observation Schedule (ADOS) assessments (Falkmer *et al.* 2013). Since not everyone has access or can afford a multidisciplinary team, it is still recommended that the ADOS and/or ADI-R be included in the assessment.

Although it may be complicated for counselors working in addictions to ensure an appropriate screening for autism, it is important to consider doing so since the SUD treatment protocols and outcomes can be very different for those with ASD than those with, say, ADHD (Kronenberg *et al.* 2015; Sizoo *et al.* 2010). For instance, individuals with undiagnosed ASD and SUD appear to receive less familial and social support than those who receive an official ASD diagnosis:

> The SUD + ASD clients mainly report that if their family and friends had known about the ASD earlier, they might have been more supportive... I was able to explain why, in my opinion, I did things the way I did so now the bond with my family is much stronger than it used to be. (Kronenberg *et al.* 2015, p.245)

IS IT ADDICTION? FOR AUTISM SPECIALISTS, FAMILY MEMBERS, AND SELF-ADVOCATES

For those working with adolescents and adults with an autism diagnosis, it is hard to recommend a particular screening for drug and alcohol misuse, and if a standard assessment needs to be tailored for those with autism. There appear to be no studies regarding the effectiveness of any particular alcohol and/or drug screening for those with an autism diagnosis. There are over 75 different assessments for alcohol and drug abuse and dependence (Allen and Wilson 2003), and screenings can range from 1 to over 150 questions.

- A single question assessment for illegal drug use, "How many times in the past year have you used an illegal drug or used a prescription medication for nonmedical reasons?" has proven to be effective in general healthcare settings (Smith *et al.* 2010, p.1155).

- A one-two question assessment for adolescents during doctors' visits is recommended by the US' National Institute on Alcohol Abuse and Alcoholism: "In the *past year*, on *how many days* have you had more than a few sips of beer, wine, or any drink containing alcohol?" with the follow-up question: "If your friends drink, *how many drinks* do they usually drink on an occasion?" (NIAAA 2011).

- The CAGE approach (Ewing 1984) is often recommended for screening both adults and adolescents due to it being simple and straightforward:

  ○ Have you felt the need to *Cut down* on your drinking?

  ○ Do you feel *Annoyed* by people complaining about your drinking?

  ○ Do you ever feel *Guilty* about your drinking?

  ○ Do you ever drink an *Eye-opener* in the morning to relieve shakes?

  Two or more affirmative responses suggest that the client is a problem drinker.

- Medical professionals in community health settings are also highly encouraged to implement the broader Screening, Brief Intervention, and Referral to Treatment (SBIRT) (SAMHSA 2017b). This consists of:

  ○ *Screening*—a healthcare professional assesses a patient for risky substance use behaviors using standardized screening tools. Screening can occur in any healthcare setting.

  ○ *Brief Intervention*—a healthcare professional engages a patient showing risky substance use behaviors in a short conversation, providing feedback and advice.

  ○ *Referral to Treatment*—a healthcare professional provides a referral to brief therapy or additional treatment to patients who screen in need of additional services.

- An online tool can be another effective screening option for self-advocates, practitioners, and family members. The "Am I Alcoholic Self Test" found on the National Council on Alcoholism and Drug Dependence website (2015), and others like it, have been recommended by autism professionals. Although these online surveys are usually composed of "yes" or "no" questions, for clients, therapists, and/or loved ones filling one in together and then discussing the results can have a significant impact: "I helped the individual understand and answer the questions. The outcome of this session seemed to have a big effect for this client" (Glenna Osborne, personal interview, March 17, 2017).

These assessments and others like them may be effective for individuals with autism, although one professional working with adults with autism noted that she avoids "yes" or "no" questions, and instead offers an option of specific answers for her clients to choose from:

> If I think that drinking may be a problem for them, rather than asking, "Is drinking too much a problem for you?" I would ask (and often write):
>
> • I feel buzzed or drunk 2 or fewer times a week.
>
> • I feel buzzed or drunk 3 to 5 times a week.
>
> • I feel buzzed or drunk more than 5 times a week.
>
> I would ask them to choose which one fit the best, and then I would ask follow up questions in a similar way. If one of the options I give doesn't fit, they typically tell me it doesn't... (Glenna Osborne, personal interview, March 17, 2017)

Some researchers speculate that individuals with autism who drink or use illegal drugs can seem more "normal" when they are using; this is why screening is critical, and another reason why individuals with ASD may be underdiagnosed (Lalanne *et al.* 2015).

POSSIBLE SIGNS OF A DUAL AUTISM/ SUBSTANCE USE DIAGNOSIS

Although screening should be routine, limited funding and services may interfere with implementation; clinicians, coaches, educators, and family members may want to be made aware of possible red flags of substance use.

• Any legal or criminal complications for the individual with ASD might warrant some follow-up questions regarding the use of alcohol and illegal drugs in connection to whatever charges were filed, even if the charges do not appear to be drug- or alcohol-related.

- Another scenario worth exploring is if the client/loved one has a source of income and is running out of money unusually fast, and is unable to account for how they are draining their funds. Families may inadvertently enable their children, as one campus coach supporting students with ASD shared in a story of a college-aged client with an ASD and SUD:

Often, he would have a crisis whether it be losing his room key, needing money immediately to pay a bill, or having his meds and xbox "stolen" from his room. I eventually suspected that he was selling his drugs to others or using them too much and partying too much which is why he always needed money. His mom would always send money, and when he couldn't get more prescription meds, she would ship hers to him. This floored me. (Laurie Nederveen, personal communication, December 2, 2016)

Not all findings may lead to substance abuse, but the questions could expose a variety of other costly behavioral addictions such as gambling, gaming, role-playing, sex hotlines, pornography websites, etc. Exploring unexplained money problems might also expose whether others are exploiting the individual with an ASD.

- Another covert sign of a substance use problem might be references to new friends or dropping names after social events that do not seem familiar. It is always worth investigating these comments a little further, without seeming too intrusive.

- Other signs are unexpected or unusual mood swings or shifts in energy during a single day, such as acting tired and unmotivated, and then suddenly being revved up and excited.

- Even well-known signs that someone may be covering up drug use, like wearing a long-sleeved shirt on a hot day to conceal needle marks, may not be explored if the individual has a diagnosis of autism; sporting unseasonable clothing may be attributed to sensory issues or quirky behavior and so go unchecked.

- The same may be true if articles around the house are missing; family members might chalk this behavior up to poor executive functioning, but the absent items may actually be a means to purchase alcohol or drugs.

- With easy internet access, it is important to no longer assume individuals with limited social interactions have not learned the strategies adolescents often acquire from one another, such as stealing pills from the medicine cabinet or watering down bottles of vodka.

There is a difference between supporting and enabling. Once it is discovered that a loved one or family member has a problem with substance use, families need to take some time and figure out the best course of action. No one can force an individual to stop using substances, and the old-school "tough love" approach has been proven ineffective (Miller *et al.* 1995). Before seeking treatment, families and loved ones need to be accurate and honest with themselves, as well as with the individual with an ASD/SUD. Often, parents of a child with an ASD have worked hard for years to ensure their child has a successful transition into adulthood. After a childhood of hurdles, families may want to minimize any obstacles that may arise for their adult children, but with substance abuse, treatment is key, and should not be ignored, since waiting will only make recovery more difficult, as noted by an ASD specialist hired to assist a college student with autism:

> This student abused alcohol, marijuana, and prescription drugs. He had been unsuccessful in one or two higher education programs and was trying to make it at college... The entire family had very little knowledge of either ASD/SUD and they did not really want to focus on it. I was initially told the issue was only with alcohol and it was not a problem anymore but the student should keep clean and try to focus on going to school with this new chance... It really agitated me that the person who could have helped him the most was enabling him to stay in this pattern... I think he ended up in another college in Boston (the city that is known for their drinking), and so I can only imagine what the outcome of that was or where he is.
>
> He was a nice kid and had potential but I was not the correct support for him and the only reason I took the case was because it was presented to me that he would be the appropriate candidate and just need to maintain sobriety through community AA meetings.

I am sure this type of enabling and lying happens a lot in families. This was my only experience and I have no idea of the inception of how the substance abuse began for this particular case. (Laurie Nederveen, personal communication, December 2, 2016)

Support is offering love, encouragement, and assistance to the individual with an SUD. It is setting limits while at the same time making oneself available. Support does not mean subsidizing the person using, but it does mean allowing them to feel safe. This kind of support allows the person with an addiction to reach out when they are ready to seek treatment. Enabling is minimizing or pretending the problem doesn't exist.

SEEKING TREATMENT

Given the minimal amount of research regarding substance use in connection to an autism spectrum diagnosis, it is eye opening to see the browser search from typing in *autism and substance use*. The number of websites offering drug and alcohol rehabilitation services catering specifically to those with ASD seeking treatment is surprising. Family members, providers, loved ones, and self-advocates need to use caution when choosing a facility, however, as many of these facilities charge large amounts of money for treatment that may not be the right fit.

- Ask what treatments the facility offers that specifically address ASD, and have follow-up questions ready. When investigating services customized for individuals with autism for this book, the representatives from facilities that claimed to cater to the ASD population were unable to provide the specific treatment modalities.

- Try typing in similar internet searches and following up. A search of *Bipolar and substance abuse* and *OCD and substance abuse* generated the same treatment referral websites as the search of *Autism and substance use*. This is not to say these and other inpatient and outpatient addiction providers will not be helpful for someone with an autism diagnosis; it is just a recommendation to apply due diligence when referring a client or loved one.

- Thoughtful websites might not translate to thoughtful treatment. Though some of the information on addiction treatment websites is accurate, like the benefits of treatments such as CBT (a generic statement for most any mental health/substance abuse dual diagnosis), and the potential difficulty group sessions might present for someone with an ASD, make sure to ask questions about the facility's fit. For example, the treatment center may not require group therapy (group therapy might increase anxiety for someone with an ASD), but they may have patients share rooms overnight (which may also increase anxiety). Many of these treatment centers are quite costly, and like any major investment, thorough vetting should take place before making a major financial commitment.

How does one pick treatment services that are the right match?

- As with any treatment, it is recommended that the client or family member start with the recommendations of trusted professionals: a doctor or pediatrician, therapist, counselor, teacher, job coach, etc.

- When looking for assistance, remember that each person with a substance use diagnosis may respond differently to the various treatment modalities available to them.

- There is currently no evidence-based treatment for treating substance use for those with an autism diagnosis, but options that work for both can be recommended. On the US' Substance Abuse and Mental Health Services Administration's website, it offers a database of different approaches to treat substance dependence, ranging from inpatient rehabilitation to peer support groups (SAMHSA 2017a).

- Usually treatment providers recommend an amalgam of treatments to match the patient's needs.

- The most common treatment for adults and adolescents with ASD or SUD is a combination of medication, peer support, and residential or outpatient counseling (SAMHSA 2016b).

- Providers may need to consider collaborating with other agencies and services in order to match their patients up with the "custom-made" comprehensive services tailored for the individual with an ASD/SUD. For instance, providers from both autism and addiction services may need to collaborate with one another to ensure the patient is getting treatment in an inclusive and effective manner.

- Case managers may need to consider a variety of wrap-around services including coaching, vocational support, social skills training, and appropriate peer support (NIDA 2016). Slayter and Steenrod (2009) recommend that when providers collaborate, they "engage in conversations about the service paradigm in which they function to build 'cross-cultural' competency (i.e., the differences that might arise in collaboration between agencies that focus on fostering self-determination in community-based life vs. either a harm-reduction or abstinence-only approach)" (Slayter and Steenrod 2009, p.85).

- SUD, like autism, is managed, not cured. For addiction, relapses are often a hallmark of the diagnosis. Be prepared for these relapses. If the same modalities of treatment have been offered over and over with minimal success, consider another course of action, if possible. It is critical to remember to factor in relapse as part of treatment, rather than failed treatment.

MEDICATION OPTIONS

Medications can be an important part of treatment, especially in conjunction with counseling and other services. Proper medication management can be effective when the patient collaborates with the practitioner prescribing the medications (Deegan and Drake 2006).

- When deciding on prescription medications to treat individuals with SUD, the current protocol is to target the underlying anxiety, depression, sleep disturbances, or other issues that can co-exist, contribute, or exacerbate their condition. Drugs commonly prescribed are antidepressants, sleep aides, antipsychotic medications, and antianxiety medications.

- One reason for both SUD and ASD providers to assess for alcohol and illicit drugs is the possible interactions of medications. Although it is hoped that the patient won't relapse, relapse is common and needs to be considered when prescriptions are suggested. It may be best to avoid certain medications if there is the potential for relapse. For example, certain psychotropic medications when mixed with alcohol can be a lethal combination (Slayter and Steenrod 2009).

- Given the high levels of anxiety of many individuals on the spectrum, another concern is the use of antianxiety medications known as benzodiazepines (or more commonly, "benzos") such as Valium, Xanax, Klonopin, and Ativan (though these names are fairly well known, self-advocates and their supports should be aware that there are many other benzodiazepine medications with less familiar names):

  ○ Benzos can be habit forming. It is important to check with the prescriber or pharmacist if the antianxiety medication prescribed might be addictive, since there is evidence to warrant concern for abuse.

  ○ If a benzodiazepine is prescribed, it is important for the individual with an ASD to monitor their use carefully, and that practitioners and loved ones assist to ensure the individual with an ASD is adhering to the prescribed dosage.

- There are also medications (both long-acting shots or daily pills) such as naltroxone and Campral that target substance abuse, reducing cravings for alcohol or opioids by diminishing the rewards that alcohol and illegal drugs might offer. These are not the same as Antabuse, an oral medication that induces negative consequences such as nausea and vomiting if an individual drinks alcohol.

- There are also effective maintenance options for opioid dependence such as methadone or buprenorphine (Suboxone or Subutex).

- Certain facilities may not allow for particular prescriptions. The patient's treatment placement plan needs to be considered when prescribing. Either the treatment facilities or the prescriptions may need to change, depending on which will be the more effective or valued course of action for the patient.

Just like the general population, individuals with autism can respond to medications differently, so it is important that if a new medication is prescribed, the individual receiving treatment be carefully monitored.

PEER SUPPORT

Alcoholics Anonymous or Narcotics Anonymous are ever-present, and therefore the habitual recommendations for those with a substance use diagnosis. A common mistake made outside and within the substance abuse community is conflating counseling with peer support. AA and NA are not therapy; they are peer support groups, and should be recommended in conjunction with other treatments such as therapy. Despite the distinction, AA/NA are often the go-to referrals for those with an SUD; courts and employers often conditionally mandate AA or NA. Many individuals with autism have done well with AA and NA given its structure and built-in peer support, but not everyone thrives in big groups, especially if they have social anxiety or do not understand the rules. One individual on the spectrum who benefited from AA explained:

> Another visual metaphor which is helpful in a number of ways is trellises that plants grow on—if you've ever seen morning glories growing up corn stalks—by their nature some plants can stand on their own easily like corn...some other plants can't; they have to have something that they climb up. That doesn't mean there is anything wrong with that plant, it's just in their nature. As long as they have something to hang on to then they can thrive. What their hanging on to that trellis doesn't do the growing for them but it provides a structure that it's possible to wrap around and then they do the work of growing and then they grow. AA provides that structure for me both as an alcoholic and as a person with autism. There's a structure that won't do the work for me but makes it possible for me to structure my life around so that I can then—with support—do things I never would be able to do without support. And it doesn't mean there's something wrong with me for me to need support. I accept it as part of my nature. The interdependence and the opportunity for interconnection recognizing the commonality, if you will in AA terms, the common spiritual ground that we all have. (Anonymous, personal communication, November 7, 2016)

For others, it may be difficult to understand:

The hardest thing was helping him [a client with autism] go through the 12 steps. He couldn't understand what they wanted him to do with the material from the meetings. He was willing to do the 12 steps, but didn't understand the 12 steps.

AA is very social, and it's not conducive for a person with autism. They often don't know when to talk. The court tells them they have to go and they don't understand how it works. (Mike Chapman, personal interview, January 17, 2017)

There are many alternative peer support groups to AA and NA, such as Self Management and Recovery Training (SMART), Rational Recovery, Women for Sobriety, and Celebrate Recovery. The advantage of AA is that it is familiar, and it is ubiquitous. In the US, one can find a meeting almost anywhere, anytime; there is no other support group like it. If an individual with an addiction is in crisis in the US, and in many other countries throughout the world, they can contact AA and someone will reach out to them and, in most cases, will get them to a meeting. Though officially AA is peer support, it is still considered a treatment modality, and despite mixed results, is commonly referred or mandated as treatment. For some, AA has saved their lives, and for others, it has felt detrimental for a variety of reasons. The AA philosophy of "powerlessness" may not be the right choice for those with an autism diagnosis since they may already feel powerless—powerless to fit in, powerless against bullies, and powerless to change (Szalavitz 2016). Matt Tinsley, co-author of *Asperger Syndrome and Alcohol: Drinking to Cope?* (2008), shared that AA was not a good match for him:

...as a non-churchgoer and non-believer in organized religion [AA] didn't appeal to me at all. I had never felt comfortable attending AA meetings in the past and felt there was an air of cult about them. They didn't seem to be open to the ideas of anyone who challenged them. Those who advocated other methods of treatment were told that AA was the only method of staying sober that was proven to work. (p.94)

If peer support like AA/NA is offered in conjunction with treatment, it could definitely add a layer of defense to an individual's recovery, but it shouldn't be a required component of treatment for everyone.

SUD COUNSELING OPTIONS

There are a range of interventions targeting different aspects of substance use and autism. For instance, counseling is generally recommended for adolescents and adults who have a diagnosis of either ASD or SUD, especially if it is accompanied by depression and/or anxiety (Autism Speaks 2010; NIDA 2016).

- There are several evidence-based behavioral therapies for SUD, but the most common are:

    ○ Twelve Step Therapy, derived from the Twelve Steps of AA.

    ○ Contingency management, designed to provide incentives to maintain sobriety.

    ○ Motivational enhancement, which works with the patient to build on their ambivalence and build on what has motivated them to reach out and seek treatment.

    ○ Cognitive behavioral therapy (CBT) was initially crafted for the treatment of anxiety and depression, teaching patients to be aware of the stressors or situations that might cause them to turn to substance use. Although its efficacy varies depending on the substance treated, it has proven to be successful when treating cannabis and nicotine dependency (Hofmann *et al.* 2012).

    ○ Family behavior therapy is particularly effective for adolescents and young adults, and brings the family into counseling to address the larger family dynamic rather than just an individual's relationship to addiction (NIDA 2012; SAMHSA 2016b).

- Currently, there are few evidence-based therapies for adolescents and adults with autism, as this field appears to still be "in its infancy" (Bishop-Fitzpatrick, Minshew, and Eack 2014, p.325). Adding an SUD can only make finding the proper treatment modality more daunting. "SUD can be difficult to treat with a neurotypical client. In my experience, due to often co-existing illogical thinking styles, and a desire to 'be like everyone else' it can be more difficult when working with a client with ASD.

Having said that, I usually try to rely on CBT" (Mitchell Nagler, personal communication, February 22, 2017).

- CBT has proven to be an effective treatment for individuals with ASD without co-occurring SUD, and is often the recommended treatment (with adaptations) for individuals on the spectrum for emotion regulation (Spain *et al.* 2015). "This [CBT] focuses on changing behaviour and is very concrete and logical, which suits the autistic mind better than more emotion-based psycho-analytic therapies" (Tinsley and Hendrickx 2008, p.88). It would stand to reason that CBT with the requisite adaptations might be the best treatment modality for someone with ASD and SUD, although there is no evidence yet to back this speculation. CBT's effectiveness is summed up by Matt Tinsley, an adult with ASD and SUD, when talking about the rehab facility he attended:

This therapy aims to make one examine one's thoughts and change them if they are "faulty," e.g. if one tends to generalize, or if small detail tends to cloud one's entire perspective. The link is made between the thoughts and feelings that may lead to addictive behaviour. By challenging these thoughts and the feelings associated with them, this behaviour can be amended. By coincidence, this seems to be the best therapy for those on the Autistic Spectrum. (2008, p.94)

TREATMENTS THAT ASD AND SUD HAVE IN COMMON

Both disorders require long-term treatment and involve multiple parts and levels of both specialized treatment facilities, primary health services, and support in the primary health services... to date, no specific guidelines for clinicians working with these patients have been published; thus, these individuals have to rely on clinical expertise and common guidelines for the two disorders. (Arnevik and Helverschou 2016, p.74)

For example, group therapy is the most common form of treatment for those who have a substance use diagnosis, but individuals with an ASD appear to benefit from one-on-one treatment, and so, as should always be the case when treating substance use and/or an ASD in any individual, interventions need to be fitted to the particular patient

(Arnevik and Helverschou 2016). What will work for one patient may not be helpful for another, as was noted in a study of autism and substance use: "Although generally recommended in the treatment of alcohol use disorder, group therapy was felt not to be an effective intervention for this patient" (Rengit *et al.* 2016, p.2516). The authors go on to share that the patient (with both ASD and SUD) might gain some much-needed social exposure via group treatment, but given the downsides of group treatment, such as increased social anxiety, vulnerability to the influences of others, an inability to keep up and add to rapid conversation, and the lack of overall social skill that might be expected of a group participant, the group approach may not be warranted (Rengit *et al.* 2016).

According to several studies, harm reduction might be more effective for someone with an ASD and an SUD than total abstinence. As Kronenberg *et al.* (2015) found, many patients preferred controlled substance use in order to interact socially as well as reduce tension and agitation. Clinicians may want to remain open to the possibility of reducing substance use rather than abolishing it in order to maintain the patient's self-determination as well as increasing the potential for "buy in" to treatment.

> More specifically, Mr. A was given more control over the frequency and duration of therapy appointments (meeting for 20 or 30 min and every other week); appointment times were kept consistent (same day and time) and structured similarly, starting with initial agenda setting, review of anxiety and mood scores, discussion of alcohol use over the prior week, administration of a Breathalyzer test (Mr. A would often remind the therapist if he forgot), and then finally a "check out" which included goal setting for the week and a discussion of something unrelated to his alcohol use... Overall, therapeutic goals were kept meaningful to him and manageable, short-term (1–2 weeks ahead) in duration, and concrete and limited to Mr. A's priorities... (Rengit *et al.* 2016, p.2517)

Having the patient participate and assist in creating a treatment plan is a lot less common in substance use treatment than it could be. Since the majority of substance use treatment programs are modeled on the Twelve Steps of AA, there is the expectation that the patient "get with the program" rather than the program getting with the patient. By not plugging their patient into typical SUD treatment protocols and instead, taking into account the nuances of his ASD, Rengit *et al.* (2016) were able to allow their patient control, which in turn encouraged engagement. The patient's engagement in the act of harm reduction offered treatment and at the same time, empowerment:

> Mr. A took responsibility for goal tracking i.e. reporting his alcohol intake per week using a computerized alcohol use monitoring log. Mr. A liked data, figures, and the ritual of tracking and would email this chart to the therapist prior to each session. This also allowed him to demonstrate his computer competency skills fostering his self-esteem. (Rengit *et al.* 2016, p.2517)

Interestingly, Rengit *et al.* go on to note that Mr. A reduced his drinking substantially, but never gave it up entirely. This may not be possible for everyone with an SUD, but the all-or-nothing thinking that often accompanies recovery may not always be the best way to address an individual's substance use.

TREATMENT DELIVERY OPTIONS

The decision about how treatment is delivered should be made in conjunction with the patient, if possible. There are a host of options that can vary depending on an individual's socioeconomic status, their cultural background, geographic locale, or how long the patient has been grappling with drugs or alcohol:

- Individual or group counseling in an outpatient setting. The advantage of this treatment is that it allows the person being treated for SUD to remain in the community with their current supports in place.

- Inpatient or residential treatment is offered when living in the community might be too risky, and/or if an individual may need broader behavioral issues addressed. There are various types of residential options: long-term can range from six months to two years, and short-term can range from two weeks to ninety days. Short-term facilities are more common and aim to offer intensive treatment so that an individual can transition back into the community. Long-term treatment is effective if an individual has started using substances at a very young age, and needs time to relearn how to function without substances in the community.

A caveat regarding long-term inpatient treatment—due to deinstitutionalization, it may not be available for those with ASD who have co-occurring intellectual challenges. Residential SUD treatment provided by government-run facilities may likely reject an application by someone with an ICD precisely because of laws put in place to prevent the warehousing of adolescents and adults with intellectual challenges (as was done in the past). Private options may still be available, but finding the right setting may be trickier than for individuals with ASD without co-occurring ICD.

• Halfway or three-quarters houses, such as an Oxford House, offer a semi-residential option where the individual is in the community living with others in recovery.

If someone has relapsed over and over, and the same actions are taken for their treatment, it might be time to try a different approach. For instance, if short-term residential care proves to be ineffective, long-term residential care might be a good match. For some, leaving familiar surroundings may be detrimental, but for others, getting away from their hometown might be an asset. It might also be worth looking into the studies currently being offered by reputable agencies such as the National Institutes of Health (2017a). Though evidence-based treatment is currently the rallying cry of the mental health community, a new and possibly helpful treatment can only become evidence-based via trials. Checking what reputable clinicians are currently researching could be a viable option for treatment. The only caveat is the possibility that the patient would be assigned to a control group rather than the treatment protocol, although sometimes, participants from the control group are offered the option to try the intervention after the study is completed, if the treatment protocol proved advantageous.

ADDRESSING THE GLOBAL NEEDS OF THE DUALLY DIAGNOSED

What little literature there is on SUD and ASD seems to focus on the global needs of those with an ASD. This may mean that controlled substance use is important to their personal recovery. Individuals with co-occurring autism and substance dependence are often simply trying "to live a normal life," and using substances to reduce the symptoms of their ASD such as anxiety or awkward social behaviors (Kronenberg *et al.* 2015, p.246). This is not a call for unchecked substance use among those with an autism diagnosis, but for some, controlled substance use may make their lives manageable.

> What I have always understood is that a drink helps calm me down somewhat and makes me more at ease in social situations: it has helped me as someone with Asperger syndrome (AS) to feel "normal".
> What I didn't know, as I was not [self] diagnosed until my mid-thirties, however, was that this was partly due to my condition. Having a drink in social situations lessened my nerves and relaxed me in general. It also helped to provide downtime from the awareness of being "different." (Johnson 2017)

As with the neurotypical population, drinking to ease social stress is acceptable; it is only when the individuals over-indulge or become dependent on alcohol that there should be concern. But the standard approach of "all or nothing" when it comes to substances may leave the patient with an ASD feeling they've given up their only known support for anxiety. In certain circumstances, allowing the patient to take control and reduce their substance intake systematically may be more effective.

The literature suggests that the most effective treatments for SUD are those that target a range of concerns, not just the substance (Laudet and White 2010; SAMHSA 2016b). Laudet and White (2010) find that addressing comprehensive treatment can have a significant impact on recovery outcomes. It is recommended that a variety of services are offered, addressing:

- employment
- housing
- relationships
- various environmental and social factors.

The same is true for adults with ASD. Rather than focusing solely on behaviors, it is critical to address:

- employment

- relationships

- daily living skills

- independence.

(ASHA 2017)

Glenna Osborne, from the Transition to Adult Services at the UNC TEACCH Autism Program, found that working with the client on a combination of schedules and calendars, social narratives, Twelve Step recovery worksheets as well as personalized worksheets proved helpful for her clients who were trying to maintain abstinence from alcohol and marijuana.

- The main focus of the TEACCH approach is to provide highly structured support for individuals with an autism diagnosis.

- Many in the SUD field believe that a highly structured approach may be effective for the majority of their clients as well (Center for Substance Abuse Treatment 2005).

The goal is to provide organized systems that allow the individual with an ASD/SUD to identify positive alternatives to replace getting high, while at the same time, exploring strategies for avoiding relapse.

For example, a TEACCH counselor and patient crafted a structured list of specifically tailored strategies for the client ("B") to work on each week, limiting and structuring the choice options, and allowing the client to keep records of his actions to share and review with his counselor.

The first week the list might have ten items, and read like this:

- We reviewed how B needs to RANDOMLY choose an item and then go to do it. B needs to do the item chosen even if he does not feel like he wants to do the item. We discussed that it is important to make sure the item is randomly chosen. B will choose and do something at random from the bag. R and B will continue to work on how to use the grab bag. *There is space on this list for B to write. He has penned in: call a friend, games of solitaire, fiction writing, play a video game, visit the library. Each entry is accompanied by the date he did the activity.*

- B will continue to role-play calling H and others, including the [alcohol] HOTLINE as if he has an urge to drink. He will do this at least two times a week. Practice calling different people and practice leaving voicemail. *B has written the names of people he practiced with along with the date: Dad, Glenna, other family members and friends, as well as the actual hotline.*

- B will continue to use a calendar to write positive things to help him feel that he can overcome the alcohol challenges in his life. B will continue to do this every day. B can get new ideas from other sources as needed. B can look on the internet for "positive quotes"...

- B will continue to exercise several times a week. R can help B learn new exercise routines. B and R can come up with new exercise routine on the computer—like a spreadsheet...

(B's notebook 2009)

The list goes on, offering pragmatic exercises with achievable goals. The counselor has also set up a calendar for B.

- B's calendar has a space below it where he glued pictures he's found online or in magazines that have some personal significance: some smiley emoticons, mugs of coffee, and images of the sun breaking through clouds.

- A simple schedule is noted for each day's breakfast, lunch, and dinner that are checked off after they are completed. On the back, B has written a different positive statement for each day: some were from a list given to him, some are adaptations from AA, some he came up with or he elicited from family members.

11/16 – I work hard to overcome my challenges.

11/17 – I'm a great person many people enjoy meeting.

11/18 – I want to be aware to be able to experience the wonderful parts of life!

11/19 – I can let go of problems and turn them over to my higher power.

11/20 – I am reliable...

(B's notebook, 2009)

Each month has a slew of positive statements. This is a modified form of CBT teaching B to engage in a concrete strategy to create positive *self-talk*: "5/26 – I'm willing to make difficult decisions to help my recovery" (B's notebook, 2009).

Having a counselor to work with B to adapt the language and intent of the Twelve Steps into something meaningful is particularly helpful, since B did not feel comfortable going to meetings.

For individuals with an ASD, psycho-educational approaches, such as having structured, visible support like a calendar and/or schedule may offer predictability and comfort (Hume and Odom 2007). Though the efficacy of adapting this model for adults does not appear to have been studied, it may be a possible strategy for treatment.

Another strategy used for individuals with an ASD is the Social Story™ or, for the adult with an ASD who is co-writing, it could be referred to as a *social narrative*. A Social Story™ is a short written description that addresses a particular skill, feeling, or situation in order to allow social inclusion in various settings (Gray and Garand 1993). Invented by Carol Gray, the structure is "picture the goal, gather the information and tailor the text" (The National Autistic Society 2017). A social narrative is a blend of a Social Story™ and real-life moments written by the person with autism with the assistance of a counselor.

In the case of B (previously discussed), he and his counselor could construct narratives to address particular situations and circumstances that B might encounter. He could then put the narrative in his notebook to review when he needed to:

Feeling Resentful when Other People are Drinking

In the past, I have felt resentful at times when other people have a glass of wine or a drink and I cannot drink. Recently I have felt resentful about my dad having a glass of wine at dinner.

It will be helpful for me to think about myself as being "allergic" to alcohol, like other people are allergic to seafood or peanuts, etc.

I can learn not to feel resentful about this so that my family and friends can enjoy what they want to enjoy.

I also can sometimes ask for a "virgin" or non-alcoholic drink. (B's notebook, 2009)

This story addresses a recent scenario, confirms and validates the patient's feelings about such scenarios, and offers strategies to address these sorts of situations that may be helpful. This approach can reduce the stress of particular encounters for the individual with an ASD, possibly alleviating stress prior to and during uncomfortable social situations for those with an autism diagnosis (Autism Society 2015a). It should be noted that Social Stories™ are effective for children, but it is unclear if they have a similar impact on adults. But it seems intuitively helpful to anyone with an SUD or ASD to write out detailed, specific, and personalized narratives regarding their relationship to drugs or alcohol, the impact it may have on them and others around them, and the narratives can also offer concrete strategies to address possible emotions and actions.

OTHER CONSIDERATIONS FOR INDIVIDUALS WITH AUTISM AND SUBSTANCE USE

An important consideration when trying to engage an individual with an ASD in treatment for SUD is to keep in mind the relationship individuals with either an autism or addiction diagnosis might have with the medical community. People with addictions, an already marginalized group, feel particularly stigmatized seeking substance abuse treatment, especially if they have many repeat visits (Luoma et al. 2007). Even though the general consensus is that substance use is an illness or disability, treatment providers in healthcare may have negative attitudes toward patients with SUDs: "A study among general practitioners also showed that patients with drug abuse problems are often perceived as manipulative, aggressive, rude, and poorly motivated" (van Boekel et al. 2013, p.30).

Many individuals with an ASD, particularly those who have an undiagnosed ASD, might have had a lot of prior experience with healthcare providers and have felt misunderstood (Lewis 2016). Chances are, by the time someone with autism is grappling with an SUD, they have already had contact with the healthcare system, and may well have had negative experiences:

> ...I was hospitalized for having what was labeled a "psychotic episode." I started falling further into my depressive state, further

exacerbated by the fact that those who believed they were helping me were unwilling to listen to me. I felt like I was talking to a brick wall. Even after getting a neuropsychological test, my doctor and therapist still kept trying to apply labels that didn't fit. (Attwood et al. 2014, p.297)

As explored earlier in this book, it is highly likely that individuals with an ASD initially started using substances to self-medicate. If this is the case, it stands to reason that they may be suspicious of treatment and/or providers as they may have sought treatment and understanding in the past and didn't find relief, and so, self-medicated. Family members, professionals, and self-advocates need to carefully negotiate with one another in order to maintain that critical balance of seeking appropriate treatment while allowing for self-determination. It is important to remember that the individual with the dual autism/SUD diagnoses may have:

- sought relief many times in the past and not found it

- not received a proper diagnosis until recently (if at all)

- been actively misdiagnosed more than once

- been blamed by professionals and family members due to misdiagnoses.

As a result of these experiences, the individual may have a mistrust of treatment options if others in the past have been ineffective (due to misdiagnosis), or mistrust "institutions" in general. They may have concerns about having a formal record of a diagnosis, and doubt that there would be any benefits to being diagnosed (Lewis 2016).

Although the face of autism has often been presented as a white child with extensive familial support, this is not always the case. People of color have autism, and many individuals with an ASD of any race may not have the support of their families, particularly if they also have a substance use diagnosis. It is important to keep in mind the micro and macro impact of these two diagnoses in terms of:

- mental and physical health

- stigma

- social support

- cultural connections and disconnections

- socioeconomic status

- housing

- employment

- relationships.

These are a few examples of the multitude of possible circumstances and feelings that might be linked to an individual with an ASD/SUD, such as an inability to afford treatment, poor money management, high anxiety, distrust of professionals, being exploited, minimal familial support, homelessness, and on and on.

SUBSTANCE ABUSE PREVENTION

According to Autism Speaks (2017c), in recent years the rates of autism have risen 10–17 percent annually. Given the steady climb of autism diagnoses over the past 20 years, there will be a significant increase in adults with autism.

> Some sources cite that roughly 80 percent of those individuals with autism are under the age of 22. Given that the prevalence of autism has increased 10-fold during the past decade, the number of children with autism who will become adults over the next few years is huge. Some call it the "autism Tsunami." (AFAA 2014)

As mentioned earlier in this book, many of these adults identified with autism at an early age might have received enough support and services to be expected to enter into the workforce and live independently. The risks of this wave of adults with an ASD using substances are about the same or, given current research, maybe even higher than neurotypical adults. How do we prepare for this?

Just as early intervention is critical in achieving favorable outcomes for individuals diagnosed with autism, early intervention toward prevention is equally important in reducing the risk for developing a substance use problem (Office of the Surgeon General 2016). The Surgeon General's report (2016, p.3-1) emphasizes that:

> ...it is critical to prevent substance misuse from starting to identify those who have already begun to misuse substances and intervene

early. Evidence-based prevention interventions, carried out before the need for treatment, are critical because they can delay early use and stop the progression from use to problematic use or to a substance use disorder.

- Parental involvement with children with autism cannot be an assumed protective factor if the caregivers are not directly addressing the risks of using alcohol and illegal drugs.

- It is never too early or too late to address substance use. Parents and caregivers can begin to address substance use when their children are little, so by the time children are paying more attention to their peers' actions in adolescence, the individual with an ASD may have already internalized the information offered, and will be able to navigate new social rules and hurdles (Office of the Surgeon General 2016).

- It is fair to assume that an adolescent with autism may struggle socially, not understand the unspoken social rules, and have difficulty relating to their peers (Raising Children Network 2013). Although these social complications may reduce peer pressure, they may increase the desire for the ability to fit in and socialize with ease (NIDA 2014a).

- On the National Institute on Drug Abuse's list (2014a), after *to fit in*, the next two indicators of potential substance abuse among teenagers are *to feel good* and *to feel better*, which may definitely put an adolescent with ASD, particularly one who doesn't feel good because they do not fit in, at risk.

- Providers and family members of adolescents with an autism diagnosis need to monitor no differently than they would for typical teens.

- Though alcohol and drug prevention is targeted to adolescents, now that individuals with ASD are attending college and entering the workforce, active prevention needs to continue past adolescence.

In the college setting, they came to the program because it is known to support college students with ASD. Being on a college campus is definitely a variable that makes drugs and alcohol more available. However, whether in the campus setting or in my private practice, what I hear most often is that they begin to use it [drugs or alcohol] to "fit in." (Mitchell Nagler, personal communication, February 22, 2017)

There are currently three categories of preventative interventions:

- *Universal,* aimed broadly at a general population.

- *Selective,* aiming for a subgroup that may be at high risk.

- *Indicated,* targeted to those already using substances but who have not developed a substance use problem.

Given that research is evolving at a rapid rate regarding the risks of certain populations to develop an SUD, and that families may not be aware of genetic risks that may already be at play, universal intervention seems warranted, though a mix of all three should be made available as needed (Office of the Surgeon General 2016). An example of a universal intervention is setting a minimum drinking age, criminalizing driving while intoxicated, or reducing the availability of substances. Given the current opioid crisis, it is shocking to think that the same universal interventions applied to other illicit substances have not been assigned to prescription opioids, despite calls to do so.

The number of prescriptions for opioids (like hydrocodone and oxycodone products) have escalated, from around 76 million in 1991 to nearly 207 million in 2013, with the US their biggest consumer globally, accounting for almost 100 percent of the world total for hydrocodone (e.g., Vicodin) and 81 percent for oxycodone (e.g., Percocet) (NIDA 2014b).

Teenagers are encouraged to engage in athletics, in some instances, pushed into sports so it will look good on college applications, yet they are not monitored for what they are prescribed if they incur an injury. "I cannot tell you the number of patients I have that are currently addicted to heroin who say their addiction began after being prescribed Percocet or Vicodin as the result of an injury in high school or middle school" (Elizabeth Kunreuther, March 30, 2017). Of course, given the rate of prescribed opioids, a teen doesn't have to do sports to have access. American medicine cabinets are storing vials of opioids left over from minor surgeries, dental work, or orthopedic procedures. Many teens with addictions confess they started by raiding their parents' or their friends' parents' medicine cabinets. A surprising intervention has Nalaxone, a rescue medicine for opioid overdoses, in middle and high school nurses' offices (Harris 2017). States are currently backpedaling to put limits on how opioids are prescribed (NGA 2016). As mentioned in previous chapters, teenagers and adults with autism are not immune to the opioid epidemic. Families need to be aware that their family members with autism can get caught up in these large-scale issues that impact a significant swath of the population. A positive outcome of the opioid crisis (other than the huge financial gains for those invested in big pharma) is the call for compassionate treatment and interventions.

- In the community, currently, there are a number of evidence-based programs that can be implemented to a broad base in order to reduce the risk of substance abuse, from classroom-centered interventions to pediatric practices as well as community outreach.

- The interventions may bolster life skills, address harm reduction, strengthen families, increase self-confidence, introduce effective critical thinking, or teach proper listening skills.

- It is unclear if these preventative educational interventions may need to be adapted for those with an autism diagnosis, but since there are commonalities, such as impaired social skills, these prevention strategies could well offer effective outcomes.

... specific rehabilitative programmes on social cognition and the affective component of empathy in particular, would be key elements of the therapeutic project on Addiction to reinforce the patient's interpersonal skills. These programmes would promote empowerment of the interpersonal skills and maintenance of meaningful and secure interpersonal relationships that constitute important components of therapy. (Ferrari *et al.* 2014, p.358)

- Selective interventions may need to be adapted for the ASD community since they may be at a higher risk for developing an SUD.

- Social Stories™ addressing fitting in versus the long-term impact of drug and alcohol abuse could be woven into middle and high school exceptional children's programs.

- The first high school transition team meeting, where the individual with an autism diagnosis (by the age of 16 of younger) and their personal and professional supports meet to plan for post-high school goals, might be a good time to explore, identify, and address all the potential risks of transitioning into independence including substance use (US Department of Education 2017). Parents or providers may brush this educational opportunity aside, but opening up the discussion and addressing the risks of SUD with the whole transition team might offer the opportunity for the individual with an ASD to explore the risks of substance abuse with trusted supports. This may need to be a topic raised regularly in order to enlighten and prepare all involved to assess the protective and risk factors the child, patient, or student might encounter.

The current challenge is finding appropriate and targeted evidence-based treatments for adults and adolescents with autism. Research regarding adults with an ASD is now just starting to gain traction. Much more research and treatment is needed as the tsunami of ASD youth transitions into adulthood. Some of these treatments should focus on employment, others on independent living, and others on social competencies. Prevention is key because, as one YouTube commenter shared: "I immediately related to the self-medicate deal. Glad to see your vid [sic] man. The poor social skills and anxiety is where I struggle. Booze seems to make me feel normal relative to people I'm around" (Soluna 2016). Interventions need to address the wellbeing of the individual with an autism spectrum diagnosis, bolstering them so that they do not feel the need to reach for alcohol or illicit drugs.

CONCLUSION

As we write this book, there is only one other book addressing autism spectrum diagnosis in connection to substance use—Tinsley and Hendrickx's (2013) *Asperger Syndrome and Alcohol: Drinking to Cope?* In it, Tinsley shared he was self-medicating his undiagnosed Asperger's and using alcohol to cope. We hypothesize that for Tinsley, getting an autism diagnosis was a critical step toward recovery. This is not an uncommon assumption. In much of the literature, an autism diagnosis for an individual who has a substance use diagnosis is sometimes considered a golden ticket to sobriety. But with a generation diagnosed with autism in childhood now entering the ranks of adulthood, this is no longer the case. There are self-advocates, family members, job coaches, and other treatment providers who assert that receiving a diagnosis is not enough to end the substance use. Even getting targeted therapies for an ASD is not enough. Many argue that having an ASD diagnosis may have no impact on an individual's substance use at all. Even those who already have a diagnosis can be dubious of it being a protective factor, as noted in a vlog post from a young adult with an ASD:

> All these thoughts that go on in my brain all the time that make me so exhausted, that stop my speech from coming out properly... [with alcohol] I'm just so much more relaxed and more sociable. I can have weird conversations with people. I walk up to people and introduce myself. People think that I'm just a normal person. They treat me as an equal because everyone's weird when they're drunk, everyone. And yeah, I'm going to miss that and I can't think of anything in the world no matter how much antianxiety medication there is...or whatever that will make feel like that and it sucks. It sucks because I'm going to have to spend the rest of my

life now...just sober and so detached and I feel I work so hard...and a lot of people think that if you don't have anything interesting to say they don't give you the time of day... I don't understand how I can live like this. (Grant 2015)

Both statistics and the testimony of self-advocates, family members, and treatment providers suggest that adolescents and adults with autism struggle more in adult life than their neurotypical cohort. People with an ASD want to hold a job, but get laid off. They want to go to college, but cannot adapt to collegiate life. They want relationships, but don't fit in. The desire to fit in and the inability to do so would lead anyone to look for relief, an escape, or an excuse for appearing different.

As the autistic learns to behave more like a neurotypical, the expectations are raised. As s/he ages, society becomes less and less accepting, claiming we (autistics) are old enough to know better. No matter how well we compensate and seek to behave and communicate as expected for our age it eventually becomes impossible, and we burn out completely.

The 80% unemployment estimate for adult autistics may be necessarily an estimate, but it seems to me a very likely accurate one. Employers easily fire autistics, no matter what the law says. We don't fit in to the corporate culture, and we are often too easily manipulated and set up. Bullying is not only seen in childhood... autistic adults encounter it almost daily. (Carey 2016)

We are not prophesizing gloom and doom; we are reporting what we see. Of course there are exceptions. There are fabulous success stories that we acknowledge and celebrate, but until appropriate services, supports, and resources for all adolescents and adults with an ASD are easily accessible, the risk of substance abuse among this population will continue to be high. The combination of the prevalence of an ASD along with the particular deficits associated with the diagnosis make the current trend of developing an addiction a monumental problem.

That said, we advise parents of younger children with an ASD to pace themselves. Of course, it is highly unlikely that a parent of a young child with autism will choose to pick up this book, but we hope that those who read it spread the word. Early intervention for an ASD is indeed important, but most likely it will not be the only emotional, temporal, or financial investment made in the next 20+ years. As mentioned earlier in this book, teachers, friends, and family may eagerly rally around the young child needing assistance, but may not offer the same level of support to the teen with lanky hair and acne stimming in the back of the classroom. Early interventions offer the possibility for children with an ASD to attend school and perhaps have the opportunity to mingle with their neurotypical cohort, but it may not offer much more than that. Raising a child with an ASD can be a challenge and, for the most part, remains a challenge, despite early interventions. This needs to be said because if families and providers do not prepare, the individual with an ASD may well be at risk for a host of unexpected struggles, and we already know that substance abuse is on the list.

If the preschool years are considered the ideal period for addressing behaviors associated with an ASD, then we would like to suggest that, in order to decrease the chances of an adolescent or young adult developing an addiction, SUD interventions be targeted to middle school-aged children. Realistically, most of the effort, expense, and time will fall to family members, but the payoff, if these efforts are successful, is invaluable. During those early teen years, it may be exhausting to maintain a balance between offering protection and allowing autonomy. As with any individual prone to addiction, the key is to teach emotion regulation skills at an early age, essentially fostering the child's wherewithal so that they can cope without illicit substances. We applaud any efforts made in advance in order to steer a loved one or client away from developing an addiction.

We do not want to insult self-advocates by alerting families and providers to the struggles they may or may not encounter. Rather, we commend their hard work, tenacity, and intense desire to persevere despite significant hurdles.

We do not want to insult those struggling with an SUD because this is a group that has been stigmatized like few others. If we see addiction as a medical condition, and most do, what other illness results in punishment and incarceration instead of treatment and compassion? The absolute degradation, humiliation, and shame that this particular diagnosis brings to anyone who stumbles into it is horrifying. This makes those with an SUD a complicated population to work with. It is rare and surprising to witness individuals in pain and suffering who will readily debase themselves. Of course there are some who may accept sympathy and may even feel sorry for themselves, but on the whole, this is a population so beaten down by stigma that they are often their own jury, judge, prosecutor, and jailor—berating themselves for ending up in this situation. A common instigator of drug or alcohol use is trauma.

Once hooked, the person with the SUD may lie, cheat, prostitute, or steal to feed their habit. Often, they push away the ones they love due to shame. It is hard not to judge the actions of the person with an addiction, but it may help to see their behaviors not as intentional, but as primal symptoms of a struggle to survive.

There was a period not long ago when the language of Alcoholics Anonymous permeated our culture. People were twelve-stepping their way through grief, bad employment situations, failing marriages, and losing weight. Although AA is a lifesaver for many, its language of powerlessness and its philosophy of offering oneself to a higher power do not always translate to every situation. During the tumultuous years of the 1960s and 1970s, during the rise in civil rights, anti-war, feminist, and other antiestablishment protests, some therapists encouraged their patients to get in touch with their anger. With the advent of psychopharmacological alternatives for mental health treatment, that approach has all but disappeared. There has now been a shift to anger management and to the current trend of mindfulness. We have nothing against treatments that calm the mind and try to manage racing and tumultuous thoughts as an alternative to self-medication, but we do question whether distress, discontentment, and anger should always be medicalized as symptoms when, in fact, they may be legitimate and warranted. Feeling powerless, especially among those who may not fit in, who have been fired from their jobs for not having the right social manner, who are consistently misunderstood or dismissed for not being neurotypical, may lead anyone to turn to substances, or worse, for solace:

> I am 55 years old and have held at least 22 jobs in the past 20 years. I have no family support for ASD as well and many have ended relationships with me due to my autistic qualities. Going 50 or more years without given a chance really has made me want to leave this world much earlier. (Carey 2016)

Sometimes it is critical to be empowered and to take action and not to accept one's inherent limitations in order to move forward. We believe that it may not always be necessary to make amends and ask forgiveness or seek acceptance from an unforgiving culture. We advocate for hope, action, and tolerance for those individuals with an ASD and/or SUD. Though we have set out to tackle a particular issue that affects the autism community, reading the accounts of those with autism struggling with substance abuse or other co-occurring mental health issues not only solidified our initial goal to offer information and advice, it also imbued us with a desire to advocate.

This book is not pushing a particular theory or methodology, but we are encouraging understanding, compassion, education, and patience. If there is one takeaway from this book, it is not to make assumptions. Sometimes our culture's blind faith in authority presents information as undeniable and as *the standard* way of thinking, way of behaving, way of feeling, way of acting, but we allow that there may not be one right answer. The clinicians and doctors we were most impressed with before, during, and after writing this book were the ones who offered choices, asked the patients what they thought, and took the time to work alongside patients rather than stand over them. That is the approach we endorse. What may be the right direction for one may not be for another. If a problem presents itself, the problem itself needs be considered before a solution is explored.

Sometimes we might go into crisis mode even if it isn't necessary. If there is a concern regarding substance use, before doing the research, making the calls, enrolling in treatment facilities, and reaching for the credit card, we need to step back and think about credible goals that can be realistically achieved. With opioid use, the risk of overdose warrants a crisis mode initially, but once the person using opioids is safe in a hospital or detox facility, advocate for time to sit with the individual and consider the options. People with an addiction may not be ready to see there is a problem, or they may see a problem but see no way out of it, and that can be frustrating. The hope is there will be an opportunity to go through this process again and again until the individual, hijacked by substances, is ready to try something different. While a patient or loved one is in treatment, try to ensure they receive an accurate mental health diagnosis, not necessarily the one that someone stamped into their record some years back and that they have been saddled with ever since. Question and re-question if the individual's diagnosis is a match, if it fits, if it makes sense. And if it is a match, then look at the treatment options with hope, tempered with a critical eye.

We need to be wary of established hierarchies of thought, of unrealistic outcomes, of expectations offered by treatments. This is particularly relevant in both the autism and addiction communities.

What we have learned from writing this book is that there may be no single answer but multiple possibilities. We truly believe that the resourcefulness and tenacity we have witnessed in both the autism and addiction communities will bring about successful and impressive treatments, teachings, and policies. We look forward to being part of that movement.

REFERENCES

AA (Alcoholics Anonymous) (1952) *The Twelve Steps of Alcoholics Anonymous.* New York: Alcoholics Anonymous World Services, Inc. Accessed on February 25, 2017 at www.aa.org/assets/en_US/smf-121_en.pdf.

AA (2002) *Alcoholics Anonymous: The Big Book.* New York: Alcoholics Anonymous World Services, Inc. (Original work published 1939.)

AANE (Asperger/Autism Network) (2017) 'Asperger Profiles: Prevalence.' Accessed on February 9, 2017 at www.aane.org/prevalence.

ADA National Network (2017) 'What are a public or private college-university's responsibilities to students with disabilities?' Accessed on April 9, 2017 at https://adata.org/faq/what-are-public-or-private-college-universitys-responsibilities-students-disabilities.

ADAA (Anxiety and Depression Association of America) (2016) 'Substance Use Disorders.' Accessed on December 2, 2016 at www.adaa.org/understanding-anxiety/related-illnesses/substance-abuse.

Adreon, D. and Durocher, J. S. (2007) 'Evaluating the college transition needs of individuals with high-functioning autism spectrum disorders.' *Intervention in School and Clinic 42(5)*, 271–279.

AFAA (Advancing Futures for Adults with Autism) (2014) 'About AFAA.' Accessed on March 30, 2017 at www.afaa-us.org/about.

Alcohol Justice and the San Rafael Alcohol & Drug Coalition (2015) *Alcopops: Sweet, Cheap, and Dangerous to Youth.* Accessed on November 13, 2016 at https://alcoholjustice.org/images/reports/AlcopopsReportFinalWeb.pdf.

Alexander, B. K. (2010) 'Addiction: The view from Rat Park.' Accessed on November 20, 2016 at www.brucekalexander.com/articles-speeches/rat-park/148-addiction-the-view-from-rat-park.

Allen, V. and Wilson, J. (eds) (2003) *Assessing Alcohol Problems: A Guide for Clinicians and Researchers.* National Institute on Alcohol Abuse and Alcoholism. Accessed on March 30, 2017 at https://pubs.niaaa.nih.gov/publications/AssessingAlcohol/index.htm.

Anagnostou, E., Soorya, L., Brian, J., Dupuis, A., Mankad, D., Smile, S., and Jacob, S. (2014) 'Intranasal oxytocin in the treatment of autism spectrum disorders: A review of literature and early safety and efficacy data in youth.' *Brain Research 1580*, 188–198.

Anderson, D. K., Liang, J. W., and Lord, C. (2014) 'Predicting young adult outcome among more and less cognitively able individuals with autism spectrum disorders.' *Journal of Child Psychology and Psychiatry 55*(5), 485–494.

APA (American Psychiatric Association) (2000) *Diagnostic and Statistical Manual of Mental Disorders, Fourth Edition, Text Revision (DSM-IV-TR)*. Arlington, VA: American Psychiatric Association Publishing.

APA (2013) *Diagnostic and Statistical Manual of Mental Disorders, Fifth Edition (DSM-5)*. Arlington, VA: American Psychiatric Association Publishing.

Arnevik, E. A. and Helverschou, S. B. (2016) 'Autism spectrum disorder and co-occurring substance use disorder: A systematic review.' *Substance Abuse: Research and Treatment 10*, 69.

ASHA (American Speech-Language-Hearing Association) (2017) 'Autism: Overview.' Accessed on April 1, 2017 at www.asha.org/PRPSpecificTopic.aspx?folderid=8589935303&section=Treatment.

Aspiehepcat (2012) 'Asperger's and heroin.' Adventures in Multiple Diagnoses, Parenting and Academia. Accessed on March 24, 2017 at https://aspiehepcat.wordpress.com/2012/07/26/aspergers-and-heroin.

Aspies Central (2017) 'Addicted to weed.' Asperger's and Autism Community. Accessed on April 20, 2017 at www.aspiescentral.com/threads/addicted-to-weed.19083.

Attwood, T. (2016) 'Foreword.' In L. Jackson, *Sex, Drugs and Asperger's Syndrome (ASD): A User Guide to Adulthood* (pp.7–13). London: Jessica Kingsley Publishers.

Attwood, T., Evans, C. R., and Lesko, A. (eds) (2014) *Been There. Done That. Try This! An Aspie's Guide to Life on Earth*. London: Jessica Kingsley Publishers.

Autism Society (2015a) 'Ask the Experts: 5 Structured Social Coaching Tips for Parents and Caregivers of Children with Autism.' Accessed on March 24, 2017 at www.autism-society.org/news/ask-the-experts-structured-social-coaching-tips-for-parents-and-caregivers-of-children-with-autism.

Autism Society (2015b) 'Facts and Statistics.' Accessed on February 13, 2017 at www.autism-society.org/what-is/facts-and-statistics.

Autism Society (2016) 'What is Autism?' Accessed on March 26, 2017 at www.autism-society.org/what-is.

Autism Speaks (2010) 'How is Autism Treated?' Accessed on March 28, 2017 at www.autismspeaks.org/docs/family_services_docs/100day2/Treatment_Version_2_0.pdf.

Autism Speaks (2012) 'Educating Students with Autism.' Accessed on February 23, 2017 at www.autismspeaks.org/sites/default/files/sctk_educating_students_with_autism.pdf.

Autism Speaks (2017a) 'Asperger Syndrome: What is Asperger Syndrome?' Accessed on February 8, 2017 at www.autismspeaks.org/what-autism/asperger-syndrome.

Autism Speaks (2017b) 'Exploring autism's gut–brain connection – one microbiome at a time.' Autism Speaks. Accessed on March 3, 2017 at www.autismspeaks.org/blog/2016/11/01/exploring-autism's-gut-brain-connection---one-microbiome-time.

Autism Speaks (2017c) 'Frequently Asked Questions.' Accessed on March 25, 2017 at www.autismspeaks.org/what-autism/faq.

Autism Speaks (2017d) 'Symptoms: What are the symptoms of autism?' Accessed on February 8, 2017 at www.autismspeaks.org/what-autism/symptoms.

Autsticandproud (2013) 'i LIKE being different!' a boy with Aspergers gives some views through his eyes... Accessed on February 27, 2017 at https://autisticandproud.wordpress.com/2013/01/31/i-like-being-different.

Bates, C. (2013) 'Five disorders from depression to autism share a genetic link, which could pave the way for new treatments.' Mail Online. Accessed on February 24, 2017 at www.dailymail.co.uk/health/article-2285902/Five-disorders-depression-autism-share-genetic-link-pave-way-new-treatments.html.

Bechara, A. (2005) 'Decision making, impulse control and loss of willpower to resist drugs: A neurocognitive perspective.' *Nature Neuroscience 8(*11) 1458–1463.

Bettelheim, B. (1967) *Empty Fortress.* New York: Simon & Schuster.

Beyers, J. M., Toumbourou, J. W., Catalano, R. F., Arthur, M. W., and Hawkins, J. D. (2004) 'A cross-national comparison of risk and protective factors for adolescent substance use: The United States and Australia.' *Journal of Adolescent Health 35*(1), 3–16.

Birch, J. (2003) *Congratulations! It's Asperger Syndrome.* London: Jessica Kingsley Publishers.

Bischof, G., Rumpf, H. J., Hapke, U., Meyer, C., and John, U. (2003) 'Types of natural recovery from alcohol dependence: A cluster analytic approach.' *Addiction 98*(12), 1737–1746.

Bishop-Fitzpatrick, L., Minshew, N. J., and Eack, S. M. (2014) 'A Systematic Review of Psychosocial Interventions for Adults with Autism Spectrum Disorders.' In F. R. Volkmar, B. Reichow, and J. McPartland (eds) *Adolescents and Adults with Autism Spectrum Disorders* (pp.315–327). New York: Springer.

Blogger.com (2009) 'Marijuana as a Treatment for Autism.' Accessed on April 15, 2017 at www.blogger.com/comment.g?blogID=4841851020927689 16&postID= 4345459905 37414772.

Bollard, G. (2011) 'How does Aspergers affect Employment Prospects?' Accessed on April 18, 2017 at http://life-with-aspergers.blogspot.com/2008/03/how-does-aspergers-affect-employment.html.

Brugha, T., McManus, S., Bankart, J., Scott, F., *et al.* (2011) 'Epidemiology of autism spectrum disorders in adults in the community in England', *Archives of General Psychiatry 68*(5), 459–465.

Burgard, J. F., Donohue, B., Azrin, N. H., and Teichner, G. (2000) 'Prevalence and treatment of substance abuse in the mentally retarded population: An empirical review.' *Journal of Psychoactive Drugs 32*(3), 293–298.

Butwicka, A., Långström, N., Larsson, H., Lundström, S., Serlachius, E., Almqvist, C., and Lichtenstein, P. (2017) 'Increased risk for substance use-related problems in autism spectrum disorders: A population-based cohort study.' *Journal of Autism and Developmental Disorders 47*(1), 80–89.

Callaway, E. (2017) 'Brain scans spot early signs of autism in high-risk babies.' *Nature* February 15. Accessed on April 3, 2017 at www.nature.com/news/brain-scans-spot-early-signs-of-autism-in-high-risk-babies-1.21484.

Camarena, P. M. and Sarigiani, P. A. (2009) 'Postsecondary educational aspirations of high-functioning adolescents with autism spectrum disorders and their parents.' *Focus on Autism and Other Developmental Disabilities 24*(2), 115–128.

Cao-Nguyen, Vannee, University of West Florida Autism Inclusion Program, Personal Communication, February 24, 2017.

Carey, C. E., Agrawal, A., Bucholz, K., Hartz, S., *et al.* (2016) 'Associations between polygenic risk for psychiatric disorders and substance involvement.' *Frontiers in Genetics 7*, 149.

Carey, M. (2016) 'Where are all the old people with autism? Most of them are dead. Can we stop denying their existence and start trying to make a difference?' Accessed on April 27, 2017 at https://leftbrainrightbrain.co.uk/2016/03/18/where-are-all-the-old-people-with-autism-most-of-them-are-dead-can-we-stop-denying-their-existence-and-start-trying-to-make-a-difference.

Carpenter, S. (2015) 'For adults with autism, a lack of support when they need it most.' *The Washington Post* March 23. Accessed on February 28, 2017 at www.washingtonpost.com/national/health-science/for-adults-with-autism-a-lack-of-support-when-they-need-it-most/2015/03/23/cd082c64-b396-11e4-854b-a38d13486ba1_story.html?utm_term=.254bfdb7875d.

Caselli, G. and Spada, M. M. (2016) 'Desire thinking: A new target for treatment of addictive behaviors?' *International Journal of Cognitive Therapy* 9(4), 344–355.

Cashin, A. and Newman, C. (2009) 'Autism in the criminal justice detention system: A review of the literature.' *Journal of Forensic Nursing* 5(2), 70–5.

Cassidy C. M., Brodeur, M., Lepage, M., and Malla, A. (2014) 'Do reward processing deficits in schizophrenia-spectrum disorders promote cannabis use? An investigation of physiological response to natural rewards and drug cues.' *Journal of Psychiatry and Neuroscience* 39(5), 339–347.

CDC (Centers for Disease Control and Prevention) (1999) 'Suicide: Risk and Protective Factors.' Accessed on March 26, 2017 at www.cdc.gov/violenceprevention/suicide/riskprotectivefactors.html.

CDC (2015) 'Autism Spectrum Disorder: Signs and Symptoms.' Accessed on April 4, 2017 at www.cdc.gov/ncbddd/autism/signs.html.

CDC (2016) 'Autism Spectrum Disorder: Data and Statistics.' Accessed on April 3, 2017 at www.cdc.gov/ncbddd/autism/data.html.

Center for Substance Abuse Treatment (2005) *Substance Abuse Treatment for Persons With Co-Occurring Disorders.* Treatment Improvement Protocol (TIP) Series 42. DHHS Publication No. (SMA) 05-3992. Rockville, MD: Substance Abuse and Mental Health Services Administration.

Cermak, S. A., Curtin, C., and Bandini, L. G. (2010) 'Food selectivity and sensory sensitivity in children with autism spectrum disorders.' *Journal of the American Dietetic Association* 110(2), 238–246.

Chapman, Mike, Director of Supported Employment Services, University of North Carolina TEACCH Autism Program, Personal Interview, January 17, 2017.

Chapman, S. L. C. and Wu, L. T. (2012) 'Substance abuse among individuals with intellectual disabilities.' *Research in Developmental Disabilities* 33(4), 1147–1156.

Chen, Y. H., Liao, D. L., Lai, C. H., and Chen, C. H. (2013) 'Genetic analysis of AUTS2 as a susceptibility gene of heroin dependence.' *Drug and Alcohol Dependence* 128(3), 238–242.

Chevallier, C., Kohls, G., Troiani, V., Brodkin, E. S., and Schultz, R. T. (2012) 'The social motivation theory of autism.' *Trends in Cognitive Sciences* 16(4), 231–239.

Chowdhury, M. and Benson, B. A. (2011) 'Deinstitutionalization and quality of life of individuals with intellectual disability: A review of the international literature.' *Journal of Policy and Practice in Intellectual Disabilities* 8(4), 256–265.

Clarke, T., Tickle, A., and Gillott, A. (2016) 'Substance use disorder in Asperger syndrome: An investigation into the development and maintenance of substance use disorder by individuals with a diagnosis of Asperger syndrome.' *International Journal of Drug Policy* 27, 154–163.

Cloninger, C. (1987) 'Neurogenetic adaptive mechanisms.' *Science* 236, 410–416.

Compton, M. T., Furman, A. C., and Kaslow, N. J. (2004) 'Lower negative symptom scores among cannabis-dependent patients with schizophrenia-spectrum disorders: Preliminary evidence from an African American first-episode sample.' *Schizophrenia Research* 71(1), 61–64.

Creswell, J. D. (2016) 'Mindfulness interventions.' *Annual Review of Psychology* 68, 491–516.

Damiano, C. R., Aloi, J., Treadway, M., Bodfish, J. W., and Dichter, G. S. (2012) 'Adults with autism spectrum disorders exhibit decreased sensitivity to reward parameters when making effort-based decisions.' *Journal of Neurodevelopmental Disorders* 4(1), 1.

Davide-Rivera, J. (2012) 'The Autistic College Student and Executive Dysfunction.' Accessed on April 19, 2017 at https://aspiewriter.wordpress.com/2012/12/16/the-autistic-college-student-executive-dysfunction.

de Alwis, D., Agrawal, A., Reiersen, A. M., Constantino, J. N., Henders, A., Martin, N. G., and Lynskey, M. T. (2014) 'ADHD symptoms, autistic traits, and substance use and misuse in adult Australian twins.' *Journal of Studies on Alcohol and Drugs 75*(2), 211–221.

de Bruin, E. I., Ferdinand, R. F., Meester, S., de Nijs, P. F., and Verheij, F. (2007) 'High rates of psychiatric co-morbidity in PDD-NOS.' *Journal of Autism and Developmental Disorders 37*(5), 877–886.

de Kwant, F. (2016) 'Autism, the brain gut connection and leaky gut syndrome.' Accessed on March 3, 2017 at http://autimates.org/autism-the-brain-gut-connection-and-the-leaky-gut-syndrome.

DeAngelis, T. (2008) 'The two faces of oxytocin.' *Monitor on Psychology 39*(2), 30–33.

Deegan, P. E. and Drake, R. E. (2006) 'Shared decision making and medication management in the recovery process.' *Psychiatric Services 57*(11), 1636–1639.

Delisle, Jayson, Supported Employment Coordinator, Triangle Region, University of North Carolina TEACCH Program, Personal Communication, February 9, 2017.

Des Roches Rosa, S. (2016) 'Unbroken Brain Author Maia Szalavitz on Autism, and Addiction.' Accessed on 4/20/17 at www.thinkingautismguide.com/2016/09/unbroken-brain-author-maia-szalavitz-on.html.

Drugs-Forum (2009) 'Opiates and Autism.' Accessed on April 15, 2017 at https://drugs-forum.com/threads/opiates-and-autism.82745.

Dumont, G. J. H., Sweep, F. C. G. J., van der Steen, R., Hermsen, R., Donders, A. R. T., Touw, D. J., and Verkes, R. J. (2009) 'Increased oxytocin concentrations and prosocial feelings in humans after ecstasy (3, 4-methylenedioxymethamphetamine) administration.' *Social Neuroscience 4*(4), 359–366.

Dvorsky, G. (2012) 'How Autism is Changing the World for Everybody.' Accessed on April 23, 2017 at http://io9.gizmodo.com/5928135/how-autism-is-changing-the-world-for-everybody.

Entine, J. and Locwin, B. (2016) 'Autism in our DNA? Slew of studies points to genetics as main driver, but there is no "autism gene".' Accessed on February 12, 2017 at www.geneticliteracyproject.org/2016/07/21/autism-in-our-dna-slew-of-studies-points-to-genetics-as-main-driver-but-there-is-no-autism-gene.

Eriksson, J. M., Andersen, L. M., and Bejerot, S. (2016) 'Short Autism Screening Test.' PsychCentral. Accessed on March 14, 2017 at https://psychcentral.com/quizzes/autism-quiz.htm.

Ewing, J. A. (1984) 'Detecting alcoholism: The CAGE questionnaire.' *Journal of the American Medical Association 252*, 1905–1907.

Falkmer, T., Anderson, K., Falkmer, M., and Horlin, C. (2013) 'Diagnostic procedures in autism spectrum disorders: A systematic literature review.' *European Child & Adolescent Psychiatry 22*(6), 329–340.

Faulkner, W. (1990) *The Sound and the Fury*. First Vintage International Edition. New York: Vintage Books. (Original work published 1929.)

Ferrari, V., Smeraldi, E., Bottero, G., and Politi, E. (2014) 'Addiction and empathy: A preliminary analysis.' *Neurological Sciences 35*(6), 855–859.

Ferri, M., Amato, L., and Davoli, M. (2006) 'Alcoholics Anonymous and other 12-step programmes for alcohol dependence.' *Cochrane Database of Systematic Reviews 3*. Art. No. CD005032.

Franzwa, G. (1998) 'Degrees of Culpability: Aristotle and the Language of Addiction.' *HUMANITAS XI*(1). Accessed on December 2, 2016 at www.nhinet.org/humsub/franzwa.htm.

Galanter, M., Kleber, H. D., and Brady, K. (eds) (2014) *The American Psychiatric Publishing Textbook of Substance Abuse Treatment.* Arlington, VA: American Psychiatric Association Publishing. Available at http://psychiatryonline.org/doi/book/10.1176/appi.books.9781615370030.

Gallup, J., Serianni, B., Duff, C., and Gallup, A. (2016) 'An exploration of friendships and socialization for adolescents with autism engaged in massively multiplayer online role-playing games (MMORPG).' *Education and Training in Autism and Developmental Disabilities 51*(3), 223–237.

Gates, G. J. (2011) 'How many people are lesbian, gay, bisexual and transgender?' The Williams Institute, UCLA School of Law. Accessed on March 10, 2017 at https://williamsinstitute.law.ucla.edu/wp-content/uploads/Gates-How-Many-People-LGBT-Apr-2011.pdf.

Geeky Science Mom's Tumbler (2013) 'Special Interest, Obsession, or Perseveration? – Part 1; What is it all about?' Accessed on February 8, 2017 at http://geekysciencemom.tumblr.com/post/43418779629/special-interest-obsession-or-perseveration.

Gelbar, N., Shefcyk, A., and Reichow, B. (2015) 'A comprehensive survey of current and former college students with autism spectrum disorders.' *Yale Journal of Biology and Medicine 88*(1), 45–68.

Gelernter, J., Kranzler, H. R., Sherva, R., Almasy, L., Koesterer, R., Smith, A. H., and Wodarz, N. (2014) 'Genome-wide association study of alcohol dependence: Significant findings in African-and European-Americans including novel risk loci.' *Molecular Psychiatry 19*(1), 41–49.

Genetic Science Learning Center (2013) 'Insights from Identical Twins.' Accessed on February 3, 2017 at http://learn.genetics.utah.edu/content/epigenetics/twins.

Ghaziuddin, M. (2005) *Mental Health Aspects of Autism and Asperger Syndrome.* London: Jessica Kingsley Publishers.

Ghaziuddin, M., Weidmer-Mikhail, E., and Ghaziuddin, N. (1998) 'Comorbidity of Asperger syndrome: a preliminary report.' *Journal of Intellectual Disability Research,* 4: 279–283.

Goin-Kochel, R. P., Myers, B. J., and Mackintosh, V. H. (2007) 'Parental reports on the use of treatments and therapies for children with autism spectrum disorders.' *Research in Autism Spectrum Disorders 1*(3), 195–209.

Goldberg, R. (2013) *Drugs Across the Spectrum,* 7th Edition. Belmont, CA: Wadsworth Publishing.

Grandin, T. (2008) 'Introduction.' In M. Tinsley and S. Hendrickx, *Asperger Syndrome and Alcohol: Drinking to Cope?* London: Jessica Kingsley Publishers.

Grandin, T. and Moore, D. (2015) *The Loving Push: How Parents and Professionals Can Help Spectrum Kids Become Successful Adults.* Arlington, TX: Future Horizons, Inc.

Grant, J. (2015) 'Aspergers Vlog – Episode 2: Dealing with addiction.' Accessed on April 10, 2017 at www.youtube.com/watch?v=QxBSOa-ODhE.

Gray, C. A. and Garand, J. D. (1993) 'Social stories: Improving responses of students with autism with accurate social information.' *Focus on Autistic Behavior 8*(1), 1–10.

Green, V. A., Pituch, K. A., Itchon, J., Choi, A., O'Reilly, M., and Sigafoos, J. (2006) 'Internet survey of treatments used by parents of children with autism.' *Research in Developmental Disabilities 27*(1), 70–84.

Greenberg, G. (2013) 'The creation of disease.' *The New Yorker* April 30. Accessed on December 2, 2016 at www.newyorker.com/tech/elements/the-creation-of-disease.

Grund, J. P., Ronconi, S., and Zuffa, G. (2013) *Operating Guidelines: Beyond the Disease Model, New Perspectives in HR: Towards a Self Regulation and Control Model.* NADPI (New Approaches in Drug Policy and Interventions).

Hadland, S. E., Knight, J. R., and Harris, S. K. (2015) 'Medical marijuana: Review of the science and implications for developmental behavioral pediatric practice.' *Journal of Developmental and Behavioral Pediatrics 36*(2), 115.

Hall, Kate, Director of Operations, Autism Society of North Carolina, Personal Communication, March 29, 2017.

Hannon, G. and Taylor, E. P. (2013) 'Suicidal behaviour in adolescents and young adults with ASD: Findings from a systematic review.' *Clinical Psychology Review 33*(8), 1197–1204.

Harm Reduction Coalition (2017) *Principles of Harm Reduction.* Accessed on February 26, 2017 at http://harmreduction.org/about-us/principles-of-harm-reduction.

Harris, E. (2017) 'In School Nurse's Room: Tylenol, Bandages and an Antidote for Heroin.' *The New York Times* March 29. Accessed on April 1, 2017 at www.nytimes.com/2017/03/29/nyregion/in-naloxone-heroin-schools-room-overdose-antidote.html?_r=0.

Hawkins, J. D., Catalano, R. F., and Arthur, M. W. (2002) 'Promoting science-based prevention in communities.' *Addictive Behaviors 27*(6), 951–976.

Healthtalk.org (2016) Life on the Autism Spectrum. Accessed on July 22, 2017 at www.healthtalk.org/peoples-experiences/autism/life-autism-spectrum/autism-feeling-different-wanting-fit.

Hepola, S. (2015) *Blackout: Remembering the Things I Drank to Forget.* New York: Grand Central Publishing.

Hoffman, J. (2016) 'Along the autism spectrum, a path through college life.' *The New York Times* November 19. Accessed on February 20, 2017 at www.nytimes.com/2016/11/20/health/autism-spectrum-college.html?_r=0.

Hofmann, S. G., Asnaani, A., Vonk, I. J. J., Sawyer, A. T., and Fang, A. (2012) 'The efficacy of cognitive behavioral therapy: A review of meta-analyses.' *Cognitive Therapy and Research 36*(5), 427–440.

Hoge, M. A., Morris, J. A., Laraia, M., Pomerantz, A., and Farley, T. (2014) *Core Competencies for Integrated Behavioral Health and Primary Care.* Washington, DC: SAMHSA-HRSA Center for Integrated Health Solutions.

Hollocks, M. J., Jones, C. R., Pickles, A., Baird, G., Happé, F., Charman, T., and Simonoff, E. (2014) 'The association between social cognition and executive functioning and symptoms of anxiety and depression in adolescents with autism spectrum disorders.' *Autism Research 7*(2), 216–228.

Horizon Health Services (2014) 'Ask Horizon – What is "rock bottom"?' Accessed on January 19, 2017 at www.horizon-health.org/blog/2014/06/ask-horizon-rock-bottom.

Howlin, P. (2014) 'Outcomes in Adults with Autism Spectrum Disorders.' In F. Volkmar, S. Rogers, R. Paul, and K. A. Pelphrey (eds) *Handbook of Autism and Pervasive Developmental Disorders*, 4th Edition (pp.97–116). Hoboken, NJ: John Wiley & Sons, Inc.

Howlin, P., Goode, S., Hutton, J., and Rutter, M. (2004) 'Adult outcome for children with autism.' *Journal of Child Psychology and Psychiatry 45*(2), 212–229.

Hume, K. and Odom, S. (2007) 'Effects of an individual work system on the independent functioning of students with autism.' *Journal of Autism and Developmental Disorders 37*(6), 1166–1180.

Hutten, M. (2010) 'Aspergers teens and marijuana use.' My Aspergers Child: Help for Parents of Children with Asperger's & High-functioning Autism. Accessed on February 28, 2017 at www.myaspergerschild.com/2010/11/aspergers-teens-and-marijuana-use.html.

Iadarola, S., Oakes, L. A., Shih, W., Dean, M., Smith, T., and Orlich, F. (2016) 'Relationship among anxiety, depression, and family impact in adolescents with autism spectrum disorder and average-range IQ.' *Focus on Autism and Other Developmental Disabilities*, 1–11.

Jackson, C. (2013) *The Lost Weekend*. First Vintage Books Edition. New York: Random House.

Jackson, L. (2016) *Sex, Drugs & Asperger's Syndrome (ASD): A User Guide to Adulthood*. London: Jessica Kingsley Publishers.

James, M. (2016) 'Living in Both the "Autism World" and the "Neurotypical World".' Accessed on February 11, 2017 at https://themighty.com/2016/08/living-in-both-the-autism-world-and-the-neurotypical-world.

JAN (Job Accommodation Network) (2013) *Accommodation and Compliance Series: Employees with Autism Spectrum Disorder*. Accessed on February 19, 2017 at https://askjan.org/media/downloads/ASDA&CSeries.pdf.

Jekel, Dania, Director, Asperger/Autism Network, Personal Communication, January 12, 2017.

Jeste, S. S. and Geschwind, D. H. (2014) 'Disentangling the heterogeneity of autism spectrum disorder through genetic findings.' *Nature Reviews Neurology 10*(2), 74–81.

Johnson, M. (2017) 'Asperger Syndrome and Alcohol: Drinking to Cope.' Asperger Management. Accessed on March 23, 2017 at www.aspergermanagement.com/publications-2/asperger-syndrome-and-alcohol-drinking-to-cope.

Kaye, A. D., Vadivelu, N., and Urman, R. D. (eds) (2015) *Substance Abuse: Inpatient and Outpatient Management for Every Clinician*. New York: Springer-Verlag.

Keay, W. (2017) 'Alcoholism & Asperger syndrome' [video file]. Accessed on April 15, 2017 at www.youtube.com/watch?v=TySs0GK4IDU.

Kim, C. (May 22, 2014) 'Let me repeat myself.' Musings of an Aspie. Accessed on February 20, 2017 at https://musingsofanaspie.com/tag/perseveration.

Kim, C. (July 14, 2014) 'Asperger's Test: How We Experience the World Survey.' Musings of an Aspie. Accessed on April 23, 2017 at https://musingsofanaspie.com/2014/07/15/how-we-experience-the-world-survey.

King, C. and Murphy, G. H. (2014) 'A systematic review of people with autism spectrum disorder and the criminal justice system.' *Journal of Autism and Developmental Disorders 44*(11), 2717–2733.

Knapp, C. (1997) *Drinking: A Love Story*. New York: Random House Publishing Group.

Kolevzon, A., Mathewson, K. A., and Hollander, E. (2006) 'Selective serotonin reuptake inhibitors in autism: A review of efficacy and tolerability.' *The Journal of Clinical Psychiatry 67*(3), 407–414.

Kovács, G. L., Sarnyai, Z., and Szabó, G. (1998) 'Oxytocin and addiction: A review.' *Psychoneuroendocrinology 23*(8), 945–962.

Kozasa, E. H., de Souza, I. C. W., de Barros, V. V., and Noto, A. R. (2016) 'Mindfulness and Substance Abuse.' In A. Andrade and D. de Micheli (eds) *Innovations in the Treatment of Substance Addiction* (pp.101–117). Switzerland: Springer International Publishing.

Kozlowski, J. D. (2015) 'Park Playground Ban on Adults Unaccompanied by Children.' National Recreation and Park Association. Accessed on August 17, 2016 at www.nrpa.org/parks-recreation-magazine/2015/march/park-playground-ban-on-adults-unaccompanied-by-children.

Kronenberg, L. M., Slager-Visscher, K., Goossens, P. J., van den Brink, W., and van Achterberg, T. (2014) 'Everyday life consequences of substance use in adult patients with a substance use disorder (SUD) and co-occurring attention deficit/hyperactivity disorder (ADHD) or autism spectrum disorder (ASD): A patient's perspective.' *BMC Psychiatry 14*(1), 264.

Kronenberg, L. M., Verkerk-Tamminga, R., Goossens, P. J., van den Brink, W., and van Achterberg, T. (2015) 'Personal recovery in individuals diagnosed with substance use disorder (SUD) and co-occurring attention deficit/hyperactivity disorder (ADHD) or autism spectrum disorder (ASD).' *Archives of Psychiatric Nursing 29*(4), 242–248.

Kuzemchak, S. (2012) '8 facts about the autism diet.' *Parents Magazine.* Accessed on March 10, 2017 at www.parents.com/toddlers-preschoolers/health/autism/autism-diet.

Lalanne, L., Weiner, L., Trojak, B., Berna, F., and Bertschy, G. (2015) 'Substance-use disorder in high-functioning autism: Clinical and neurocognitive insights from two case reports.' *BMC Psychiatry 15*(1), 149.

Laudet, A. B. and White, W. (2010) 'What are your priorities right now? Identifying service needs across recovery stages to inform service development.' *Journal of Substance Abuse Treatment 38*(1), 51–59.

Leitner, Y. (2014) 'The co-occurrence of autism and attention deficit hyperactivity disorder in children – What do we know?' *Frontiers in Human Neuroscience 8*, 268.

Leweke, F. M., Piomelli, D., Pahlisch, F., Muhl, D., *et al.* (2012) 'Cannabidiol enhances anandamide signaling and alleviates psychotic symptoms of schizophrenia.' *Translational Psychiatry 2*, e94.

Lewis, L. F. (2016) 'Exploring the experience of self-diagnosis of autism spectrum disorder in adults.' *Archives of Psychiatric Nursing 30*(5), 575–580.

Leyfer, O. T., Folstein, S. E., Bacalman, S., Davis, N. O., Dinh, E., Morgan, J., and Lainhart, J. E. (2006) 'Comorbid psychiatric disorders in children with autism: Interview development and rates of disorders.' *Journal of Autism and Developmental Disorders 36*(7), 849–861.

Lindsmith, K. (2014) 'Stimming 101, or: How I learned to stop worrying and love the stim.' The Autism Spectrum: Gender, Sexuality, Culture and Life on the Autism Spectrum June 16. Accessed on February 16, 2017 at https://kirstenlindsmith. wordpress.com/2014/05/16/stimming-101-or-how-i-learned-to-stop-worrying-and-love-the-stim.

Livingston, J. D., Milne, T., Fang, M. L., and Amari, E. (2012) 'The effectiveness of interventions for reducing stigma related to substance use disorders: a systematic review.' *Addiction 107*(1), 39–50.

LoParo, D. and Waldman, I. D. (2015) 'The oxytocin receptor gene (OXTR) is associated with autism spectrum disorder: A meta-analysis.' *Molecular Psychiatry 20*(5), 640–646.

Luoma, J. B., Twohig, M. P., Waltz, T., Hayes, S. C., Roget, N., Padilla, M., and Fisher, G. (2007) 'An investigation of stigma in individuals receiving treatment for substance abuse.' *Addictive Behaviors 32*(7), 1331–1346.

MacMullin, J. A., Lunsky, Y., and Weiss, J. A. (2016) 'Plugged in: Electronics use in youth and young adults with autism spectrum disorder.' *Autism 20*(1), 45–54.

Maddox, B. B., Trubanova, A., and White, S. W. (2016) 'Untended wounds: Non-suicidal self-injury in adults with autism spectrum disorder.' *Autism 21*(4), 412–422.

Mandell, D. S., Ittenbach, R. F., Levy, S. E., and Pinto-Martin, J. A. (2007) 'Disparities in diagnoses received prior to a diagnosis of autism spectrum disorder.' *Journal of Autism and Developmental Disorders 37*(9), 1795–1802.

MAPS (Multidisciplinary Association for Psychedelic Studies) (2015) 'MDMA-assisted therapy for the treatment of social anxiety in autistic adults.' Accessed on March 2, 2017 at www.maps.org/research/mdma/anxiety/autism.

McCarthy, J. (2008) *Mother Warriors: A Nation of Parents Healing Autism Against All Odds.* New York: Penguin Group.

McCarthy, J. and Kartzinel, J. (2010) *Healing and Preventing Autism: A Complete Guide.* New York: Penguin Group.

McGregor, I. S. and Bowen, M. T. (2012) 'Breaking the loop: Oxytocin as a potential treatment for drug addiction.' *Hormones and Behavior 61*(3), 331–339.

McPheeters, M. L., Warren, Z., Sathe, N., Bruzek, J. L., Krishnaswami, S., Jerome, R. N., and Veenstra-VanderWeele, J. (2011) 'A systematic review of medical treatments for children with autism spectrum disorders.' *Pediatrics 127*(5), e1312–e1321.

Meadan, H., Halle, J. W., and Ebata, A. T. (2010) 'Families with children who have autism spectrum disorders: Stress and support.' *Exceptional Children 77*(1), 7–36.

Mesibov, G. B. and Shea, V. (2010) 'The TEACCH program in the era of evidence-based practice.' *Journal of Autism and Developmental Disorders 40*(5), 570–579.

Miller, G. W. (2016) 'R.I. opioid crisis: After son's death, they vow to change system.' *Providence Journal.* Accessed on April 12, 2017 at www.providencejournal.com/news/20160319/ri-opioid-crisis-after-sons-death-they-vow-to-change-system.

Miller, W. R., Brown, J. M., Simpson, T. L., Handmaker, N. S., *et al.* (1995) 'What Works? A Methodological Analysis of the Alcohol Treatment Outcome Literature.' In R.K. Hester and W.R. Miller (eds) *Handbook of Alcoholism Treatment Approaches: Effective Alternatives.* New York: Simon & Schuster, 12–21.

Minshawi, N. F., Hurwitz, S., Morriss, D., and McDougle, C. J. (2015) 'Multidisciplinary assessment and treatment of self-injurious behavior in autism spectrum disorder and intellectual disability: Integration of psychological and biological theory and approach.' *Journal of Autism and Developmental Disorders 45*(6), 1541–1568.

Morris, M. D., Bates, A., Andrew, E., Hahn, J., Page, K., and Maher, L. (2015) 'More than just someone to inject drugs with: Injecting within primary injection partnerships.' *Drug and Alcohol Dependence 156*, 275–281.

MSU Twin Registry (2017) 'Why twin studies?' Accessed on February 21, 2017 at http://msutwinstudies.com/why-twin-studies.

Nagler, Mitchell, Director, Bridges to Adelphi Program, Adelphi University, Personal Communication, February 22, 2017.

National Academy of Sciences and the National Academy of Medicine (2017) *Human Genome Editing: Science, Ethics, and Governance.* Washington, DC: National Academies Press.

National Autism Society (2014) *Autism – A Guide for Criminal Justice Professionals.* Accessed on February 22, 2017 at www.justice-ni.gov.uk/publications/autism-guide-criminal-justice-professionals.

National Autistic Society, The (2016) 'Meltdowns.' Accessed on January 10, 2017 at www.autism.org.uk/about/behaviour/meltdowns.aspx##changes.

National Autistic Society, The (2017) 'Social Stories and Comic Strip Conversations.' Accessed on March 29, 2017 at www.autism.org.uk/about/strategies/social-stories-comic-strips.aspx.

NCADD (National Council on Alcoholism and Drug Dependence) (2015) 'Am I Alcoholic Self Test.' Accessed on March 17, 2017 at www.ncadd.org/get-help/take-the-test/am-i-alcoholic-self-test.

Nederveen, Laurie, Campus Coach and Founder of Aspiring Aspies, Personal Communication, December 2, 2016.

Nelson, J. (2004) *Thirst: God and the Alcoholic Experience.* Louisville, KY: Westminster John Knox Press.

NGA (National Governors Association) (2016) 'Governors Unite in the War Against Opioids.' Accessed on April 1, 2017 at www.nga.org/cms/home/news-room/news-releases/2016--news-releases/col2-content/governors-unite-in-the-war-again.html.

Nguyen, V. (2013) 'How one family struggles with the financial costs of autism.' *Parade Magazine* April 25. Accessed on February 26, 2017 at https://parade.com/8465/viannguyen/how-one-family-struggles-with-the-financial-costs-of-autism.

NIAAA (National Institute on Alcohol Abuse and Alcoholism) (2011) *Alcohol Screening and Brief Intervention for Youth: A Practitioner's Guide.* Accessed on March 29, 2017 at https://pubs.niaaa.nih.gov/publications/Practitioner/YouthGuide/YouthGuide.pdf.

NIDA (National Institute on Drug Abuse) (2012) *Principles of Drug Addiction Treatment: A Research-based Guide,* Third edition. Accessed on March 24, 2017 at www.drugabuse.gov/publications/principles-drug-addiction-treatment/evidence-based-approaches-to-drug-addiction-treatment/behavioral-therapies.

NIDA (2014a) *Principles of Adolescent Substance Use Disorder Treatment: A Research-based Guide.* Accessed on March 30, 2017 at www.drugabuse.gov/publications/principles-adolescent-substance-use-disorder-treatment-research-based-guide/frequently-asked-questions/why-do-adolescents-take-drugs.

NIDA (2014b) 'America's Addiction to Opioids: Heroin and Prescription Drug Abuse.' May 14. Accessed on March 31, 2017 at www.drugabuse.gov/about-nida/legislative-activities/testimony-to-congress/2016/americas-addiction-to-opioids-heroin-prescription-drug-abuse.

NIDA (2016) 'Treatment Approaches for Drug Addiction'. Accessed on April 10, 2017 at www.drugabuse.gov/publications/drugfacts/treatment-approaches-drug-addiction.

NIH (National Institutes of Health) (2017a) 'NIH clinical research trials and you.' Accessed on April 2, 2017 at www.nih.gov/health-information/nih-clinical-research-trials-you.

NIH (2017b) 'What are the treatments for autism spectrum disorder (ASD)?' Accessed on March 22, 2017 at https://www.nimh.nih.gov/health/topics/autism-spectrum-disorders-asd/index.shtml.

Ochs, R (2016) 'Substance use and abuse added to emergency room screening.' *Newsday* March 5. Accessed on March 11, 2017 at www.newsday.com/news/health/substance-use-and-abuse-added-to-emergency-room-screening-1.11540408.

Office of the Surgeon General (2016) *Facing Addiction in America: The Surgeon General's Report on Alcohol, Drugs, and Health.* Washington, DC: US Department of Health and Human Services.

Ogburn, C. (2015) 'The relief of diagnosis: autism spectrum diagnosis in adults.' *Autism Asperger's Digest,* Feb.-Apr., 22-24.

Orinstein, A. J., Helt, M., Troyb, E., Tyson, K. E., Barton, M. L., Eigsti, I. M., and Fein, D. A. (2014) 'Intervention for optimal outcome in children and adolescents with a history of autism.' *Journal of Developmental and Behavioral Pediatrics 35*(4), 247–256.

Osborne, Glenna, Director of Transition to Adult Services at the University of North Carolina TEACCH Autism Program, Personal Interview, March 7, 2017.

Padawer, R. (2014) 'The kids who beat autism'. *The New York Times Magazine* July 31. Accessed on February 16, 2017 at www.nytimes.com/2014/08/03/magazine/the-kids-who-beat-autism.html.

Padwa, H., Urada, D., Antonini, V. P., Ober, A., Crèvecoeur-MacPhail, D. A., and Rawson, R. A. (2012) 'Integrating substance use disorder services with primary care: The experience in California.' *Journal of Psychoactive Drugs, 44*(4), 299–306.

Page, T. (2009) *Parallel Play: Growing up with Undiagnosed Asperger's.* New York: Anchor Books, Random House.

Palmer, A. (2006) *Realizing the College Dream with Autism or Asperger Syndrome: A Parent's Guide to Student Success.* London: Jessica Kingsley Publishers.

Peñagarikano, O., Lázaro, M. T., Lu, X. H., Gordon, A., *et al.* (2015) 'Exogenous and evoked oxytocin restores social behavior in the Cntnap2 mouse model of autism.' *Science Translational Medicine 7*(271), 271ra8.

Personal Genetics Education Project (2017) 'Personal Genetics – Beyond Your DNA.' Accessed on April 27, 2017 at https://pged.org/what-is-personal-genetics.

Poon, K. and Sidhu, D. (2017) 'Adults with autism spectrum disorders: A review of outcomes, social attainment, and interventions.' *Psychiatry 30*(2), 77–84.

Power, R. A., Kyaga, S., Uher, R., MacCabe, J. H., Långström, N., Landen, M., and Svensson, A. C. (2013) 'Fecundity of patients with schizophrenia, autism, bipolar disorder, depression, anorexia nervosa, or substance abuse vs their unaffected siblings.' *JAMA Psychiatry 70*(1), 22–30.

Prince-Hughes, D. (ed) (2002) *Aquamarine Blue 5: Personal Stories of College Students with Autism.* Athens, OH: Swallow Press.

Radhakrishnan, R., Wilkinson, S. T., and D'Souza, D. C. (2015) 'Gone to Pot – A Review of the Association between Cannabis and Psychosis.' In E. C. Temple, R. Hammersley, M. van Laar and R. F. Brown (eds) *Clearing the Smokescreen: The Current Evidence on Cannabis Use.* Lausanne, Switzerland: Frontiers Media SA, 1–24.

Raising Children Network (2013) 'Social Skills for Teenagers with Autism Spectrum Disorder.' Accessed on March 30, 2017 at http://raisingchildren.net.au/articles/autism_spectrum_disorder_social_skills_teenagers.html.

Ramos, M., Boada, L., Moreno, C., Llorente, C., Romo, J., and Parellada, M. (2013) 'Attitude and risk of substance use in adolescents diagnosed with Asperger syndrome.' *Drug and Alcohol Dependence 133*(2), 535–540.

Rao, P. A. and Landa, R. J. (2014) 'Association between severity of behavioral phenotype and comorbid attention deficit hyperactivity disorder symptoms in children with autism spectrum disorders.' *Autism 18*(3), 272–280.

Regan, T. (2014) *Shorts: Stories about Alcohol, Asperger Syndrome, and God.* London: Jessica Kingsley Publishers.

Rengit, A. C., McKowen, J. W., O'Brien, J., Howe, Y. J., and McDougle, C. J. (2016) 'Brief report: Autism spectrum disorder and substance use disorder: A review and case study.' *Journal of Autism and Developmental Disorders 46*(7), 2514–2519.

Ritvo, R. A., Ritvo, E. R., Guthrie, D., Yuwiler, A., Ritvo, M. J., and Weisbender, L. (2008) 'A scale to assist the diagnosis of autism and Asperger's disorder in adults (RAADS): A pilot study.' *Journal of Autism and Developmental Disorders 38*(2), 213–223.

Robertson, C. E. and McGillivray, J. A. (2015) 'Autism behind bars: A review of the research literature and discussion of key issues.' *The Journal of Forensic Psychiatry & Psychology 26*(6), 719–736.

Robinson, J. (2007) *Look Me in the Eye: My Life with Asperger's.* Lake Arbor, MD: Crown Publishers.

Roelfsema, M. T., Hoekstra, C. A., Allison, C., Wheelwright, S., Brayne, C., Matthews, F. E., and Baron-Cohen, S. (2012) 'Are autism spectrum conditions more prevalent in an information-technology region? A school-based study of three regions in the Netherlands.' *Journal of Autism and Developmental Disorders 42*(5), 734–739.

Rosie's Quest (2013) 'BOGO: Self Medicating and aspergers.' Accessed on April 16, 2017 at www.youtube.com/user/RosieTeaflower.

Rosin, H. (2014) 'Letting go of Asperger's.' *The Atlantic.* Accessed on April 7, 2017 at www.theatlantic.com/magazine/archive/2014/03/letting-go-of-aspergers/357563.

Rothwell, P. E. (2016) 'Autism spectrum disorders and drug addiction: Common pathways, common molecules, distinct disorders? *Frontiers in Neuroscience 10.*

Roux, A., Shattuck, P., Cooper, B., Anderson, K., Wagner, M., and Narendorf, S. (2013) 'Postsecondary employment experiences among young adults with an autism spectrum disorder.' *Journal of the American Academy of Child and Adolescent Psychiatry* *52*(9), 931–939.

SAMHSA (Substance Abuse and Mental Health Services Administration) (2010) 'Protracted Withdrawal.' *Substance Abuse Treatment Advisory 9*(1), 1–8. Accessed on March 22, 2017 at http://store.samhsa.gov/shin/content//SMA10-4554/SMA10-4554.pdf.

SAMHSA (2014) *Results from the 2013 National Survey on Drug Use and Health: Summary of National Findings.* NSDUH Series H-48, HHS Publication No. (SMA) 14-4863. Rockville, MD: SAMHSA.

SAMHSA (2015) 'Substance Use Disorders.' Accessed on November 16, 2016 at www.samhsa.gov/disorders/substance-use.

SAMHSA (2016a) 'Co-occurring Disorders.' Accessed on January 14, 2017 at www.samhsa.gov/disorders/co-occurring.

SAMHSA (2016b) 'Mental and Substance Use Disorders.' Accessed on March 10, 2017 at www.samhsa.gov/disorders.

SAMHSA (2016c) 'Treatments for Substance Use Disorders.' Accessed on December 12, 2016 at www.samhsa.gov/treatment/substance-use-disorders.

SAMHSA (2017a) 'National Registry of Evidence-based Programs and Practices.' Accessed on March 21, 2017 at http://nrepp.samhsa.gov/AdvancedSearch.aspx?mode=withoutcome.

SAMHSA (2017b) 'SBIRT: Screening, Brief Intervention, and Referral to Treatment.' Accessed on April 2, 2017 at www.integration.samhsa.gov/clinical-practice/SBIRT.

Schapir, L., Lahav, T., Zalsman, G., Krivoy, A., Sever, J., Weizman, A., and Shoval, G. (2016) 'Cigarette smoking, alcohol and cannabis use in patients with pervasive developmental disorders.' *Substance Use & Misuse 51*(11), 1415–1420.

Schumann, G., Coin, L. J., Lourdusamy, A., Charoen, P., Berger, K. H., Stacey, D., and Aulchenko, Y. S., *et al.* (2011) 'Genome-wide association and genetic functional studies identify autism susceptibility candidate 2 gene (AUTS2) in the regulation of alcohol consumption.' *Proceedings of the National Academy of Sciences 108*(17), 7119–7124.

Scott, M., Falkmer, M., Girdler, S., and Falkmer, T. (2015) 'Viewpoints on factors for successful employment for adults with autism spectrum disorder.' *PloS ONE 10*(10), e0139281.

Seigel, Z. (2016) 'Addiction is a learning disorder: Why the war on drugs is useless, AA undermines treatment, and addiction studies can learn a lot from autism.' *Salon* April 7. Accessed on December 12, 2016 at www.salon.com/2016/04/07/addiction_is_a_learning_disorder_the_war_on_drugs_is_useless_aa_undermines_treatment_and_addiction_studies_can_learn_a_lot_from_autism.

SFARI (Simons Foundation Autism Research Initiative) (2016) 'AUTS2: Relevance to autism.' Accessed on February 28, 2017 at https://gene.sfari.org/GeneDetail/AUTS2.

Sharpe, D. L. and Baker, D. L. (2007) 'Financial issues associated with having a child with autism.' *Journal of Family and Economic Issues 28*(2), 247–264.

Shattuck, P. T., Narendorf, S. C., Cooper, B., Sterzing, P. R., Wagner, M., and Taylor, J. L. (2012) 'Postsecondary education and employment among youth with an autism spectrum disorder.' *Pediatrics 129*(6), 1042–1049.

Shroomery.org (January 31, 2013) 'Re: Psychedelic drugs and Asperger's Autism.' Accessed on April 15, 2016 at www.shroomery.org/forums/showflat.php/Number/10828194/fpart/all/vc/1.

Shroomery.org (April 10, 2014) 'Re: Psychedelic drugs and Asperger's Autism.' Accessed on March 15, 2017 at www.shroomery.org/forums/showflat.php/Number/19000490.

Shroomery.org (January 24, 2017) 'ADHD, Autism medications and magic mushrooms.' Accessed on March 22, 2017 at www.shroomery.org/forums/showflat.php/Number/24027799.

Silberman, S. (2001) 'The geek syndrome.' *Wired 9*, 12.

Silberman, S. (2015) *Neurotribes: The Legacy of Autism and the Future of Neurodiversity*. New York: Penguin Random House.

Silva, G. (2015) 'How I became hopeful about my Asperger's in college.' Asperger/Autism Network. Accessed on February 12, 2017 at www.aanenetwork.org/blog/aane-listening-tour-disclosure-in-college.

Sizoo, B., van den Brink, W., Koeter, M., van Eenige, M. G., van Wijngaarden-Cremers, P., and van der Gaag, R. J. (2010) 'Treatment seeking adults with autism or ADHD and co-morbid substance use disorder: Prevalence, risk factors and functional disability.' *Drug and Alcohol Dependence 107*(1), 44–50.

Slayter, E. (2007) 'Substance abuse and mental retardation: Balancing risk management with the "dignity of risk".' *Families in Society: The Journal of Contemporary Social Services 88*(4), 651–659.

Slayter, E. and Steenrod, S. (2009) 'Addressing alcohol and drug addiction among people with mental retardation in nonaddiction settings: A need for cross-system collaboration.' *Journal of Social Work Practice in the Addictions 9*, 71–90.

Smith, F. (2011) 'Comments on marijuana for autism: Are you out of your mind… would you like to be?' Autism & Oughtisms. Accessed on March 3, 2017 at https://autismandoughtisms.wordpress.com/2011/07/19/marijuana-for-autism-are-you-out-of-your-mind-would-you-like-to-be.

Smith, J. (2012) 'ASPERGERS & Alcohol.' Accessed on April 18, 2017 at http://nurseteaspoons.blogspot.com/2012/06/aspergers-alcohol.html.

Smith, P. C., Schmidt, S. M., Allensworth-Davies, D., and Saitz, R. (2010) 'A single-question screening test for drug use in primary care.' *Archives of Internal Medicine 170*(13), 1155–1160.

SoberRecovery Forums (February 4, 2008) 'Aspergers syndrome.' Accessed on April 29, 2016 at www.soberrecovery.com/forums/mental-health/143188-aspergers-syndrome.html.

SoberRecovery Forums (July 5, 2008) 'Aspergers syndrome.' Accessed on August 14, 2016 at www.soberrecovery.com/forums/mental-health/143188-aspergers-syndrome.html.

SoberRecovery Forums (August 19, 2011) 'Aspergers syndrome.' Accessed on August 14, 2016 at www.soberrecovery.com/forums/mental-health/143188-aspergers-syndrome.html.

SoberRecovery Forums (June 10, 2012) 'Anyone in AA and diagnosed with autism/Asperger's?' Accessed on February 17, 2017 at www.soberrecovery.com/forums/mental-health/259222-anyone-aa-diagnosed-autism-aspergers.html.

SoberRecovery Forums (July 31, 2012) 'Anyone in AA and diagnosed with autism/Asperger's?' Accessed on April 30, 2016 at www.soberrecovery.com/forums/mental-health/259222-anyone-aa-diagnosed-autism-aspergers.html.

Solomon, A. (2001) *The Noonday Demon*. New York: Simon & Schuster.

Solomon, A. (2012) *Far From the Tree: Parents, Children and the Search for Identity*. New York: Simon & Schuster.

Soluna, M. (2016) 'Asperger's and substance abuse.' Accessed on April 16, 2017 at www.youtube.com/watch?v=I-Mt3VNl8RY.

Spain, D., Sin, J., Chalder, T., Murphy, D., and Happe, F. (2015) 'Cognitive behaviour therapy for adults with autism spectrum disorders and psychiatric co-morbidity: A review.' *Research in Autism Spectrum Disorders 9*, 151–162.

Spicer, Dave, Self-Advocate, Personal Interview, October 1, 2016.

St. Aubyn, E. (2012) *Bad News (Vol. 2)*. London: Pan Macmillan.

Sterling, L., Dawson, G., Estes, A., and Greenson, J. (2008) 'Characteristics associated with presence of depressive symptoms in adults with autism spectrum disorder.' *Journal of Autism and Developmental Disorders 38*(6), 1011–1018.

Stone, D. (1997) *Policy Paradox: The Art of Political Decision Making*. New York: W. W. Norton & Co. Inc.

Strang, J. F., McCambridge, J., Best, D., Beswick, T., Bearn, J., Rees, S., and Gossop, M. (2003) 'Loss of tolerance and overdose mortality after inpatient opiate detoxification: follow up study.' *BMJ 326*(7396), 959–960.

Strang, J. F., Meagher, H., Kenworthy, L., de Vries, A. L., Menvielle, E., Leibowitz, S., and Pleak, R. R. (2016) 'Initial clinical guidelines for co-occurring autism spectrum disorder and gender dysphoria or incongruence in adolescents.' *Journal of Clinical Child & Adolescent Psychology*, 1–11.

Szalavitz, M. (2016) *Unbroken Brain: A Revolutionary New Way of Understanding Addiction*. New York: St. Martin's Press.

Szalavitz, M. (2017) 'Autism's hidden habbit.' *The Atlantic*. Accessed on March 3, 2017 at https://spectrumnews.org/features/deep-dive/autisms-hidden-habit.

Tehee, E., Honan, R., and Hevey, D. (2009) 'Factors contributing to stress in parents of individuals with autistic spectrum disorders.' *Journal of Applied Research in Intellectual Disabilities 22*(1), 34–42.

Tietz, J. (2002) 'The boy who loved transit.' *Harper's Magazine 304*, 43–51. Accessed on January 6, 2017 at http://abrahamson.medill.northwestern.edu/WWW/IALJS/Tietz_BoyWhoLovedTransit_Harpers_May_2002.pdf.

Tinsley, M. (2017) 'Stories From the Heart: Paris, With New Eyes.' Accessed on April 19, 2017 at www.autismtoday.com/tag/asperger-syndrome-alcohol-drinking-to-cope.

Tinsley, M. and Hendrickx, S. (2008) *Asperger Syndrome and Alcohol: Drinking to Cope?* London: Jessica Kingsley Publishers.

U.S. Department of Education (2017), Office of Special Education and Rehabilitative Services, 'A Transition Guide to Postsecondary Education and Employment for Students and Youth with Disabilities.'Accessed on 6/17/2017 at https://www2.ed.gov/about/offices/list/osers/transition/products/postsecondary-transition-guide-2017.pdf.

US Department of Education (2015) *37th Annual Report to Congress on the Implementation of the Individuals with Disabilities Education Act*. Accessed on February 10, 2017 at www2.ed.gov/about/reports/annual/osep/2015/parts-b-c/37th-arc-for-idea.pdf.

US Department of Health and Human Services (2016) *Advancing LGBT Health and Wellbeing: 2016 Report of the HHS LGBT Policy Coordinating Committee*. Accessed on April 2, 2017 at www.hhs.gov/programs/topic-sites/lgbt/reports/health-objectives-2016.html.

UN Office on Drugs and Crime (2016) *World Drug Report 2016*. Accessed on December 10, 2016 at http://www.unodc.org/wdr2016/en/wdr2016.html.

van Boekel, L. C., Brouwers, E. P., van Weeghel, J., and Garretsen, H. F. (2013) 'Stigma among health professionals towards patients with substance use disorders and its consequences for healthcare delivery: Systematic review.' *Drug and Alcohol Dependence 131*(1), 23–35.

VanBergeijk, E., Klin, A., and Volkmar, F. (2008) 'Supporting more able students on the autism spectrum: College and beyond.' *Journal of Autism and Developmental Disorders* *38*(7), 1359–1370.

van Wijngaarden-Cremers, P.J.M., Brink, W.V., and Gaag, R.J. (2014) 'Addiction and Autism: A Remarkable Comorbidity?' *Journal of Alcoholism and Drug Dependence 2:* 170.

Volkmar, F. and Wolf, J. (2013) 'When children with autism become adults.' *World Psychiatry 12*, 79–80.

Volkow, N. D., Baler, R. D., Compton, W. M., and Weiss, S. R. (2014) 'Adverse health effects of marijuana use.' *New England Journal of Medicine 370*(23), 2219–2227.

Wallace, G. L., Kenworthy, L., Pugliese, C. E., Popal, H. S., White, E. I., Brodsky, E., and Martin, A. (2016) 'Real-world executive functions in adults with autism spectrum disorder: Profiles of impairment and associations with adaptive functioning and co-morbid anxiety and depression.' *Journal of Autism and Developmental Disorders 46*(3), 1071–1083.

White, S. (2014) 'School receives $2.2 million in federal funding to prepare students for integrated healthcare.' University of North Carolina School of Social Work. Accessed on April 2, 2017 at http://ssw.unc.edu/about/news/integrated_healthcare.

WHO (World Health Organization) (2000) *Guidelines for the Regulatory Assessment of Medicinal Products for Use in Self-medication.* Department of Essential Drugs and Medicines Policy. Accessed on March 10, 2017 at www.who.int/iris/handle/10665/66154.

Widmaier, E. P., Raff, H., and Strang, K. T. (2006) *Vander's Human Physiology: The Mechanisms of Body Function,* Tenth Edition. New York: McGraw-Hill Companies, Inc.

Willey, L.H. (1999) *Pretending to be Normal: Living with Asperger's Syndrome,* London: Jessica Kingsley Publishers.

William (2016) 'Knowing and avoiding triggers during heroin addiction treatment.' Accessed on February 10, 2017 at http://killtheheroinepidemicnationwide.org/2016/07/15/kknowing-and-avoiding-your-triggers-during-heroin-addiction-treatment.

Williams, Joseph, Medical Director, Addictions Detoxification Unit, UNC Health Care at WakeBrook, Personal Communication, April 27, 2017.

Woods, J. S. and Joseph, H. (2015) 'Stigma from the viewpoint of the patient.' *Journal of Addictive Diseases 34*(2–3), 238–247.

Wylie, P. (2014) *Very Late Diagnosis of Asperger Syndrome (Autism Spectrum Disorder): How Seeking a Diagnosis in Adulthood Can Change Your Life.* London: Jessica Kingsley Publishers.

Wylie, P., Lawson, W., and Beardon, L. (eds) (2016) *The Nine Degrees of Autism: A Developmental Model for the Alignment and Reconciliation of Neurological Conditions.* New York: Routledge.

Yale Child Study Center (2013) 'Pervasive Developmental Disorder – Not Otherwise Specified (PDD-NOS).' Accessed on April 4, 2017 at http://childstudycenter.yale.edu/autism/information/pddnos.aspx.

Young, L. J. and Barrett, C. E. (2015) 'Can oxytocin treat autism?' *Science 347*(6224), 825–826.

Yu, J., Evans, P. C., and Clark, L. P. (2006) 'Alcohol addiction and perceived sanction risks: Deterring drinking drivers.' *Journal of Criminal Justice 34*(2), 165–174.

ABOUT THE AUTHORS

Elizabeth Kunreuther has both personal and professional connections to autism spectrum disorder and SUD. She has worked in developmental disabilities for close to 20 years. After serving as the Intake Coordinator for the UNC TEACCH Autism Program for 11 years, she decided to go back to school and earn a Masters of Social Work from UNC's School of Social Work. With her MSW, Elizabeth has continued to work in the field of developmental disabilities as well as mental health and substance abuse. Elizabeth is currently a Clinical Instructor at UNC School of Medicine's Department of Psychiatry in the Addiction Detox Unit on UNC's Wakebrook campus. Elizabeth offers counseling, education, and follow-up services for individual patients seeking treatment for their SUDs.

Ann Palmer is a parent of an adult son with autism, an author and presenter, and a professional having worked with families for over 24 years. She was the Parent Support Coordinator at the University of North Carolina's TEACCH Autism Program where she developed a volunteer parent mentor program that provided support to over 800 families in North Carolina. She was the Director of Advocacy and Chapters at the Autism Society of North Carolina where she coordinated over 50 Chapters and support groups across North Carolina. Ann is currently a faculty member of the Carolina Institute for Developmental Disabilities (CIDD) at the University of North Carolina in Chapel Hill, training multidisciplinary graduate-level students on working with families. She is the author of three books published by Jessica Kingsley Publishers: *Realizing the College Dream with Autism or Asperger Syndrome: A Parent's Guide to Student Success; Parenting Across the Autism Spectrum: Unexpected Lessons We've Learned* (co-authored with Maureen Morrell and winner of the Autism Society of America's Literary Work of the Year); and *A Friend's and Relative's Guide to Supporting the Family with Autism: How Can I Help?*

SUBJECT INDEX

AUTHOR INDEX

Made in the USA
Monee, IL
08 December 2021

84343093R00109